SO YOU'VE GOT TEENAGE CHILDREN TOO…

By the same authors:

A Touch of Love

Other books by John Houghton:

Hagbane's Doom
Gublak's Greed
Surin's Revenge
The Healthy Alternative

So You've Got
Teenage Children
Too...

JOHN AND JANET HOUGHTON

KINGSWAY PUBLICATIONS
EASTBOURNE

First published 1989

Biblical quotations are from the
New International Version © International Bible Society 1973, 1978, 1984. Published by Hodder & Stoughton

Front cover design by Vic Mitchell

British Library Cataloguing in Publication Data

Houghton, John
So you've got teenage children too.
1. Adolescents. Interpersonal relationships with parents. Christian Viewpoints
I. Title II. Houghton, Janet
261.8'35874

ISBN 0-86065-732-9

Produced and printed in Great Britain for
KINGSWAY PUBLICATIONS LTD
1 St Annes Road, Eastbourne, E Sussex BN21 3UN by
Nuprint Ltd, 30b Station Road, Harpenden, Herts AL5 4SE.

Contents

Dear Fellowsuffering Teenager's Parent,

Do you ever feel that you'd like a bit of sympathy? A shoulder to cry on? Or just the knowledge that you're not on your own? Then welcome to this book.

We'd like to invite you to share in a few stories and ideas with us over a pint of nerve tonic. So why not curl up in the snug of your armchair, check that they're not spying on you, and comfort yourself with the knowledge that there are others out there going through the same things as yourself?

You may already feel that Jesus' words, 'Come ye apart...' have been fulfilled in your life—but not in the way that he intended! Never mind. What 'all the king's horses and all the king's men' couldn't do, we'll attempt in the course of the following pages!

We've just four qualifications for writing this book. Three of those are our own children, spanning at the moment fifteen through to twenty. The other is the decision we took back in 1968.

Having no previous experience, we decided to raise our children by the only text book we believed to be any good—the Bible. Twenty years on, we'd say the risk was well worth taking. God's wisdom has proved more than adequate for the task. In spite of many trials, our family life has been happy, secure and fulfilled. Though our personalities are strong and our ideas individual, we remain united on everything that really matters. God has blessed us with children who love him and who love us.

Teenagers are no problem to God. He loves them and knows exactly how to handle them. He's very willing to help you with yours. Hang on to that nerve tonic and we'll try to show you how!

Sympathetically yours,

John & Janet Houghton

Part One

Conflicts, Chats and Changes

1

The Ride of Their Lives

Raising children is a serious, hilarious and perplexing business—often all at once. Either way, it's the most important job any of us will ever do. If we fail here then we really have failed.

But be encouraged! There's a welcome paradox in this task. It's this: just when you feel you are failing most you may in fact be succeeding very well indeed. Here's an example of what we mean. It happened to John.

The June sun was generously bright and warm. We had been about two weeks in our new home. Before us stretched the challenging vista of new people to befriend, fresh opportunities to serve, worth-while things to do. It felt good to be in the will of God. Then the door crashed open. In stomped one of our daughters.

'Dad, can I speak to you in the garden?' she demanded.

I stiffened. When they need a lot of space, you can bet I need a lot of grace! We went outside. She was bristling like a broom head.

Halfway along the path she let rip.

'Dad, this house is terrible. It's awful! There's something bad about it. Ever since we've moved here nothing has gone right. We all hate it. I'm sure it's the wrong place. And we just wish we had an ordinary dad like other dads.

Why are you in the ministry? You've got no time for us. You're always busy. I hate it all. Why have we come here?'

I thought, 'I'm booked to take a conference series on how to raise teenagers in three weeks' time.'

Her voice rose to a nerve-shattering crescendo. 'It's absolutely terrible, Dad,' she screeched. 'I just don't know how we can go on like this. The whole family's falling apart. Don't you understand? Everything's falling apart!'

I looked back at the adjoining houses. They all had their windows open. 'Oh, Lord!' I groaned.

'Shh, don't forget we've got neighbours,' I urged. 'New neighbours!'

'Blow the neighbours,' she screamed. 'That's all you think about. What about me?'

The tirade continued for several minutes more.

I gazed at my darling daughter. Face red, jaw jutting, fists clenched; taut as a bow. And simmering with frustration. She'd been through a hard time—months of pain, operations, exams, boyfriend troubles. And now the first house move of her life.

You have to look beyond the outside. Overcome the hurtful, distorted words. Refuse the guilt that breeds despair. Reach through the barrier raised by mutually felt pain.

I stretched out my arms to her, spoke some home truths and told her I loved her. She softened, relaxed, put her arms around me. Then smiled brightly up into my face.

'Thanks, Dad. D'you know, you're the best dad on earth. You've always got time for us when we need you. Thanks ever so much for listening to me. I feel so much better now!'

I gave her a wan smile in return. 'Glad I could help,' I mumbled. 'Um, would you excuse me now? I need to go book my nervous breakdown before the surgery closes for lunch!'

I glanced up at those windows again. Hope the neighbours heard that last bit she'd said.

There's teenagers for you! One moment total disaster; you feel you've made some terrible mistake somewhere along the line, failed as a parent, lost your child for ever. The next minute you discover that everything's fine after all. You're the most successful parent that ever lived. And that earth-ripping hurricane was actually just a storm in a teacup viewed through an emotional magnifying glass.

Perhaps we should try to understand what's really going on? Time for a story. So if you're sitting comfortably....

A bedtime story for parents

Once upon a time, there was a pretty little harbour. And on its sheltered waters bobbed a rubber dinghy containing a contented young child.

Now on the shore was a lighthouse, and from its window two caring parents kept a watchful eye on their precious offspring.

This happened every day for many happy years. That is, until one fateful day when a strange, but not entirely unexpected, current suddenly took hold of the dinghy. All at once, it began to be dragged inexorably towards the harbour entrance.

As it did so, it began magically to change shape. It grew, and all sorts of bits and pieces began to poke out from all sorts of odd directions. Something was going on! The dinghy drew closer and closer to the open sea and the current grew stronger and stronger. The mother looked on, horrified. 'My baby!' she cried. 'My baby!' Dad looked very, very worried and said nothing.

The child gripped the sides of his new boat tightly, his face filled with trepidation. He shot a glance back to the security of the lighthouse and wished he was still in his little dinghy.

Then he spied lots of other children out on the high seas, all in boats just like his. They seemed all right. In fact, many of them were obviously enjoying the choppy waters. 'If they can do it, then so can I,' the child determined.

So, the harbour walls behind, the child began the ride of his life. At first he wasn't too sure of the controls, but by copying others, he soon got the hang of it—more or less, anyway. It was great. Far better than that boring old harbour with Mum and Dad always watching.

Not that he forgot his parents, of course. They were still watching, peering anxiously at the high seas. And every so often the child would cast a surreptitious glance in their direction—just to make sure they were still there. In fact, all children were doing the same to their parents. It's just that nobody wanted to admit it.

But it was acceptable to like your parents still. Well, sort of, anyway. So, from time to time, the child would come brumming back into the harbour and demand that his parents come out with him on to the open seas.

Poor parents! They'd stagger down the steps, suddenly feeling their age; climb into their own ancient power boat, and reluctantly ride out with their child.

But they got used to it after a fashion and even began to re-live something of their own younger days. Riding the waves could still be fun after all.

Then, just as all seemed to be settling down nicely, the child cried out at them, 'Go away. I don't want you with me any more. I'm not a kid. Why don't you let me live my own life? I want to do things my own way.'

Of course, his parents protested, muttered something inane about relationships and taking an interest, but to little avail. All their warnings of danger were met with a disdainful snort, and before they knew it, their child was off.

This cycle was often repeated and many were the occasions when Mum and Dad returned confused and weary to their lighthouse.

It was after one such episode that disaster struck. The child took on a wave too big for his boat, and just as his parents had predicted, over he went. In spite of their weariness, love and concern ruled the day. They raced to his rescue. Dripping wet, much sobered, they hauled him from the water.

Now you might have thought he would have learned something from that experience. Apparently not. For the very next day he was out there trying exactly the same manoeuvre all over again. How he managed to stay afloat this time, nobody knows.

This process continued for several heady years. His parents grew up very quickly! Life was hairy. Then, just as they thought they were about ready to snap, the waters suddenly calmed.

Lo and behold, their child was an adult. They watched with pride as he steered his graceful powerboat in and out of the harbour. He waved to them often now. And sometimes he even taught them a trick or two on the open seas. Life was surprisingly good.

And did they live happily ever after? Well, it depends. But very probably these particular parents did.

There ends our little story. In the following three chapters we'll try to explain what it all means.

2

The Dawn of Adolescence

Chapter 3 of the book known as Ecclesiastes informs us, 'There is a time for everything and a season for every activity under heaven.' A time to be born and a time to die; to plant and to uproot; to kill and to heal; to tear down and to build; to weep and to laugh; to mourn and to dance; to scatter and to gather; to embrace and to refrain; to search and to give up; to keep and to throw away; to tear and to mend; to be silent and to speak; to love and to hate; to war and to be at peace.

Note the categories well; the whole lot seems to happen to teenagers all at once! So dramatic are the changes taking place in their lives that it's nothing to find them lurching from love and peace to impending World War Three in no more than a matter of minutes.

A teenager can come off the phone having just mended someone's broken heart and immediately proceed to rip yours to shreds. That irritated refusal to lend a pen to a brother or sister can be instantly followed by a decision to send all their worldly wealth to the relief of Third World poverty. Sullen silence can as easily flip into a non-stop stream of hyperactive one-way conversation embracing world politics, a new hair dye, the ultimate meaning of life and the Maths teacher's latest girlfriend, all in the same breath.

What makes it so frustrating is that these fluctuating moods are largely beyond both their control and ours. The reason for this is simple. They are undergoing some of the most dramatic changes they will ever experience, not only in their bodies but also within their emotions and their environment. And if we protest that we were not as bad as that when we were their age, it is probably because a change is taking place in our own lives, too. It's called middle-aged loss of memory!

Body building, begin!

The dawn of adolescence is announced by the vibrant ringing of a biological alarm clock. The glands awaken. From their portals pour forth hordes of hormones eager to commence the work of transforming a child into an adult. Never is a task more zealously, more thoroughly, accomplished than by these tireless labourers.

Within little more than three or four pubescent years they can stand back to admire their masterpiece. The little girl has become a woman; the boy a man. Together they could found a dynasty.

This activity is usually greeted by a mixture of apprehension and enthusiasm on the part of the human building site that constitutes your child. Girls develop a certain coyness about their bodies, but at the same time they want you to measure their busts. They worry about the irregularity of their periods, but let it be known in a very grown-up manner that it's their 'time of the month'. Boys get embarrassed by their spontaneous erections, but they want you to feel their burgeoning biceps. They peer anxiously at their rudimentary moustaches while celebrating in full, raucous voice the transition from cracked falsetto to basso fortissimo! Both sexes worry unceasingly about their spots.

How well our children manage these changes depends to a large extent on how we have taught them to view their bodies. If the very fact of having a body is considered to be a bit of an embarrassment, something we don't talk about, then your child is likely to have difficulties in coping. Similarly, if the process of change is accompanied by dire warnings about lascivious men and uncontrollable urges then your child will grow up plagued by unwarranted guilt and fear.

On the other hand, if we as parents respond positively by encouraging and admiring our children's development, if we explain what is happening and assure them that they are normal, then it will be a time of great joy for all concerned. The ability to do this depends on us having a healthy regard for our own bodies.

Sadly, many parents don't. In spite of having lived with their bodies all their lives, they still haven't made friends with them. Maybe they've never liked the shape, or they are ashamed of what they've done with it, or what it does to them. Perhaps they feel it has too many leaks and smells, a bit like an old-fashioned plumbing system. Or possibly they believe that it is, by its very nature, sinful. And all these attitudes they may have picked up from their own parents in the first place.

Jesus had a body just like ours. His plumbing system was standard issue human grade. He had the same biological needs and urges that we have, and he went through adolescence the same as all teenagers. The only thing he didn't do with his body was use it for sinning.

The Son of God showed us that it is neither sinful nor shameful to have a human body. Hence, the redemption he offers not only sets us free from the guilt and power of actual bodily sin but also promises to release us from unwarranted guilt and shame concerning our bodies. If we have real peace about our own sexuality, we will be well-equipped to help our children into a healthy regard for theirs.

There's just one qualification we want to add to this. Freedom from shame isn't the same as a lack of modesty. Children have the right to some personal privacy. In our desire to help them accept their bodies, we mustn't force them into situations where they might feel immodest. For example, they have the right not to be seen naked or partially dressed if they so wish. We should respect that by not barging unwanted into bathrooms or bedrooms. Modesty is a virtue.

Those hysterical hormones

The suspension system on the average car consists of two components—springs to absorb the bumps, and shock absorbers to damp the recoil of the springs. Without the latter, every bump would cause your car to oscillate wildly, so much so that the occupants would soon become sea-sick!

The problem our teenagers have is that their emotional shock absorbers are not yet functioning properly. Quite simply, they do not have sufficient experience of life to moderate their feelings, so almost any bump is going to start them oscillating. The bigger the bump the bigger the bounce! And before long everyone is sick of it, your child included.

'Why do I keep crying?' is a question many parents face from their children around the ages of eleven to thirteen. 'Why do they also burst out in wild laughter for no apparent reason?' is one that we ask ourselves!

It has a lot to do with those busy hormones.

Poor men! What they go through once a month, especially if they've got daughters as well as a wife. Premenstrual tension starts long before a girl has her first period. In fact, you can more or less date when that will be in the month by plotting those tearful, tense and edgy times. And, whether her periods are regular or erratic, pretty well every month it will be the same, world without end.

Nothing changes. Way back in the book of Genesis, Rachel, hiding some stolen idols by sitting on them, produced the watertight excuse for not being able to arise when her father came looking for them. She just said, in the feminine poetry of the Authorised Version, 'The way of women is upon me.' (Pity about the prosaic NIV rendering, 'I'm having my period.') No man argued with her!

Seriously though, most women appreciate some comfort and support at these times. It's tempting, for men especially, simply to retreat to the potting shed until the storm is over. But a loving husband and father will offer sympathy and a shoulder to cry on as necessary. It's part of what the apostle Peter meant when he wrote to husbands, 'Be considerate as you live with your wives' (1 Peter 3:7).

Periods are a reality of life for most girls from puberty onwards. Some cope better than others. The reasons for this are complex and have to do with matters ranging over a girl's individual metabolism, her outlook on life, how old she is, whether or not she's had children, current stresses and strains, and the state of her health.

There is some evidence that the physical side can be helped by the addition of B-complex vitamins to the diet. Going on the Pill is also a useful way of stabilising periods, but with this other matters obviously have to be taken into consideration.

It will greatly help if you can teach your daughter not to accept the popular view that periods are the curse. It just isn't true. Periods are a God-ordained cleansing of the body in preparation for childbirth. Hence, though inconvenient, they should be looked upon as a reminder of the greatest gift he has given to us, the ability to reproduce ourselves.

Although we're not advocating that girls should take to their beds with the vapours as in a Victorian melodrama, nonetheless, the modern view that women should charge through life with their bodies and emotions strictly under control is both unreal and is a denial of something essentially, preciously feminine. For a girl to feel vulnerable and sensitive is no shame. It is part of what it means to be a woman.

God usually finds it easier to get through to us when we're feeling weak. Not only does he help us in our weaknesses but he also often has special words for us. It's good then to encourage our girls to pray about their periods and to listen sensitively to the voice of the Lord at those times.

Hormonal changes, also to some degree cyclical, affect boys somewhat differently. True, on occasions they cry inexplicably as well, but they're more likely to become morose during these times. Beware—they can rip the doors off their hinges! You say, 'Be careful,' but they don't know what you're talking about. Sullen strength, inner seething without knowing why, is difficult to live with—not to say hazardous.

You never quite know when this emotional terrorism is going to erupt. Without warning the door will crash open, the house shudder, and the family cat will bolt for safety beneath the sideboard. In stalks your son, face glowering, eyes ranging for a suitable target. It's you or the sofa. If you're sitting on the sofa at the time, it's both!

The bomb explodes. Out pours an irrational flood of highly-charged words, the force of which leaves you temporarily speechless. Your innocent sofa gasps under the pummelling of your son's fists. Then just as suddenly it's over. He retreats to the hills leaving you shell-shocked and, like your poor old sofa, wondering what on earth you have done to deserve all this.

It's male hormones! Attack and withdraw. The shock absorbers aren't yet functioning properly. Pray for the day when things settle down, and don't buy a new sofa until they do!

Boys and girls are affected by their hormonal changes. Both will have their histrionics at times; but both will also on occasions withdraw completely.

'Why are you always sitting in your room? Have we got leprosy?' you protest. They can't tell you. Why did you sit in your room when you were their age? Sometimes our children withdraw for no other reason than that they feel temporarily blue because of their see-sawing hormones. At such times, coping with normal, balanced, reasonable people like us is the last thing they can stand!

To be or not to be?

Our modern teenagers are the most media-manipulated, socially-stereotyped and peer-pressured individuals in all history. As a result, they are faced with having to make a phenomenal number of decisions, many of which will affect not only what they'll do but also who they'll become.

'Hey, teenager. What's your lifestyle going to be? Are you going to study, or not? Chosen your exam options yet? You going to work or go on the dole? When are you going to get a girlfriend? Condoms or the Pill? Where do you buy your gear? What do you think of Sexbusters' new single? You ain't gonna vote, are you? Why don't you leave home? You're not religious, are you? How do you know you're not gay? Bought any shares yet?'

One of the very salient points made by the social commentator, Alvin Toffler, is that overchoice can lead to panic, mental breakdown and ultimately apathy.

We needed to buy a new jug-kettle recently—a fairly simple task we thought. But there are dozens of the wretched things! They all look more or less the same, yet you know they can't be. Otherwise there wouldn't be so many different models. Would there? So which is the best?

They have high wattage and low wattage, balls that go up and down, two balls that go up and down, colour co-ordinated or plain white—with a pastel hint, designer-shaped or functional lines, big ones, small ones, fuel-miser ones, lights that go on when it's boiling, lights that go off when it's boiling, switches that glow in the dark, plugs that self-eject in emergency; kettles that cure all known diseases, that self-destruct in the event of nuclear war or petty larceny, that resolve your love-life and do all the housework for you. If only we could find one that would boil water!

After a bemused hour spent gazing at all these options we just clung to one another, exhausted, gibbering, vacant-eyed wrecks of what were once noble human beings. We would have welcomed with open arms the men in white coats at that point—or at least a nice cup of tea!

The effect can be similar on our children when they confront the barrage of options available to them. With little experience of life, in a culture which despises traditional wisdom and which is in any case changing rapidly, they must decide their own futures. Not surprisingly many show symptoms of premature stress. Many others find that they simply don't know their own minds, so are for ever chopping and changing their opinions. Sadly, many more lapse into apathy. They merely conform to mediocrity, taking the path of least resistance—and least hope.

Some children manage choices very well. That may be because they are born with naturally decisive temperaments; it is more likely to be because of the way in which certain other factors operate in their lives. We'd like to mention the four most important. They form a simple acrostic.

Peers
Identity
Counsel
Knowledge

Peer pressure can lead to wrong decisions, but a supportive peer group can bring great security, a sense of team work in the game of life. Hence, it's important to guide our children into the right kind of peer company. Lone children find decision-making that much harder.

Choosing friends isn't easy; choosing good friends is even harder. It's something that requires much prayer on our part.

A church youth club can come into its own at this point. If it's properly run, it can provide a wonderfully secure and creative environment in which the kids are used to discussing and advising one another on how to make up their minds.

Identity crisis has become a modern piece of jargon, used to cover everything from 'Who am I?' to 'Where shall we go for our holidays?' What matters for our children is that they should feel good when they think about themselves. Self-acceptance comes from within, from knowing that you are loved by God and by others. It arises from an acceptance of one's limitations and an appreciation of one's assets. If our children have been steadily and realistically encouraged throughout their lives, they are unlikely to undergo anything that can really be called an identity crisis. They will be well placed for making decisions.

There is widom in taking *counsel,* provided those offering it are reliable. The teenager who can communicate easily with wise, loving parents has a tremendous advantage over one who can't. We can't stress enough the importance of being available to our children.

Again, a good church has much to offer. Teenagers should feel that they have free access to pastors and youth leaders, as well as other older Christians. We parents mustn't feel our noses are being put out over this. Often a child needs to speak with someone who is less emotionally involved than we are.

By *knowledge* we don't simply mean facts, rather a grasp of the truth about life itself. What's it for? Where am I going? If our children are given proper reference points they will find their way much better across the map of life. Unfortunately, our present society has substituted relative values in place of truth. It makes the reference points more like drifting balloons in an ocean of drowning people than signposts for the wise wayfarer. That makes it even more vital for us to teach our children the fundamental truths about God and his design for our lives.

We've noticed that although most parents anticipate difficulties arising from change in the early teenage years, fewer seem prepared for another crisis point around the age of seventeen. Yet this is a particularly difficult moment for many children. It's the time when they're perhaps leaving school, wondering about work, under examination pressure. Do they go to college, university, technical college, stay on at school? Do they get married? Who do they vote for? Do they go into debt by taking on loans? Should they learn to drive? Be prepared for some interesting discussions!

We mustn't blame our children for what isn't their

fault. They are changing and they can't help it. The pressures, physically, emotionally and socially are considerable. They need our support and understanding, not simply our reaction to their reactions.

We must encourage our children that God is in control of their lives. Psalm 31:15 says, 'My times are in your hands; deliver me from my enemies and from those who pursue me.'

Teach them that their teenage years, tumultuous though they seem, are in God's hands. When they're trying to make decisions about their careers, when there's too much homework, when they've got in such a social whirl that they can't keep up with it, their times are in God's hands. And so, mercifully, are ours.

3

You Must Change with Them

This may come as a bit of a shock. You've got your husband and wife act together, the rent/mortgage is almost bearable, you feel settled in your job and are just beginning to enjoy some of those little comforts in life that make it all seem worth while. You may even feel relieved that your children are now old enough not to need you every five minutes of the day. Ah, bliss! You can relax, indulge in what you most want to do, settle down into your cosy, Dralon-lined rut.

Not a bit of it! We have to change along with our teenagers. Otherwise we will lose them, and live to regret it.

Change is always uncomfortable, especially when we're just beginning to hope for domestic peace. It's made more so by the fact that we're not so young as we were. We're usually at least in our thirties by the time our kids hit their teens. We may be in our forties or even fifties.

On top of that, the domestic bliss we desire is often counterbalanced by this being a time of life when fathers are working hard for the promotion that will make their middle years secure. For many Christians it's also a period when church may involve considerable lay leadership responsibilities.

Then you look at your kids and their culture. You freeze with horror! Whatever happened to the Beatles, Elvis and the Who? The generation gap, as we used to call it, now begins to make itself culturally felt. We aren't so 'with-it' as we used to be and we're not sure we have the energy to start trying to understand an alien youth culture, where promiscuity isn't even a dare tinged with guilt but a matter-of-fact way of saying goodnight.

How then must our role change? What must happen to those former guardians of the harbour?

A lighthouse

We must become a lighthouse to our teenagers. Jesus said,

> You are the light of the world. A city on a hill cannot be hidden. Neither do people light a lamp and put it under a bowl. Instead they put it on its stand, and it gives light to everyone in the house. In the same way, let your light shine before men, that they may see your good deeds and praise your Father in heaven (Matthew 5:14).

It is ever so important that we 'shine' before our teenagers because at no other time in life are they looking so perceptively at our lifestyle as now. Even when we're not aware of it, perhaps especially then, they are observing with a critical eye the way that we live. Their sensors are searching for even the slightest whiff of hypocrisy.

Sometimes they will be quite openly critical of us, pointing out our faults, challenging our dearest held values, ridiculing our ideas. They will ask difficult questions about our faith, and you may be tempted to think they're going to reject Christianity wholesale.

It's very tempting to react. We can start criticising them in return, knock their newly-emerging values. 'Call that music? You're not going out looking like that, are you?

How can you be so naïve? Any fool with an ounce of common sense knows better than that. Your room's like a pigsty!' And so on. It's a sure recipe for disaster and a flagrant invitation to open rebellion.

The questions our children have, even the criticisms, do not imply that they are automatically rejecting everything we have ever taught them. Indeed, the opposite. It's a sign that they are taking the challenge of our lifestyle seriously. What they're doing is testing to see whether our values are any good. Can they stand up to real questions? Are they sufficient for another, different generation?

Here's a typical example. Young Gilly comes home to her happily-married mum. 'What's the point of marriage?' she exclaims. 'All everyone does is get divorced. Why go through with it? It's more honest just to live together.'

Immediately, Mum panics. 'What about all we've taught her?' she wails. 'Is our daughter going to start sleeping around? Perhaps she is already and this is her way of letting us know.'

But ask where the idea came from. The answer is usually obvious: either a school teacher who doesn't know any better than to teach that weary old ethic from the sixties, or schoolmates whose own parents have broken up, or some commercial teenage magazine/radio station that rattles on glibly about 'honesty' in relationships.

We've heard it all before—it's what we were taught. Only in our youth the ideas were still fresh; now they're just foolish.

But don't go on about it like that just now. A 'sane lecture' will evoke some response like, 'You just don't understand,' and Gilly will probably storm off to her room.

Better to say, 'Yes, dear,' and, 'Well, I still love Daddy very much,' and leave it at that. There are times for serious discussion, of course. But not now.

From this time on, if not before, Gilly is watching her parents' marriage. She will compare it with the marriages, or lack thereof, of her friends' parents. The answers to her questions are demonstrated before her eyes—you don't have to be *un*married to be in love!

Some of the questions they ask can be very difficult to answer. It's made worse by the fact that they may not have sufficient experience even to appreciate the answer. What are we to do? Ask for divine wisdom, of course. Don't just quote scriptures or clichés—that goes almost without saying. But a lot of the time it's not so much the answer they're interested in, as the manner in which we respond. They know better than we what's happening when we react intensely by raising our voices or laying down the law. It's like the prompt found in the margin of the preacher's notes—'Shout loud, argument weak!'

Better to be a lighthouse than a foghorn!

A powerboat

Our children need our companionship. There are times when they really want us to ride the waves with them.

Sometimes they want us to go shopping with them. With boys or with girls it can be a terrifying experience! You instinctively head in the direction of C & A's or Marks & Spark's. They hate both. So you are dragged, protesting feebly, into Bums 'n' Boobs Lovemachine, an overpriced emporium characterised by pounding rock, wild flashing strobes and freakish sales assistants dropping fag ash over the racks of garish tat that passes for modern fashion. You suddenly feel about ninety years old and, worse still, have that terrible feeling they're all looking at you and wondering why Gran or Gramps was brought here in the first place.

Your kids love it. They try on this and that, want to know what you think, totally ignore your inane mumblings, want *you* to try it on and laugh loudly at the result! At the end of the day you come out, having spent all the family allowance for the week on one tatty bit of rag that they're going to wear for about two days before they hate it—just like you said in the first place!

What have you done to deserve all this, you ask as you reach for another handful of tranquillisers? Ah, but you're riding with them and that's the important thing. Companionship is worth the cost.

Discussing careers is another powerboat area.

When John was at school he had to fill in a careers form, and he put down nuclear physicist or mountain guide. He didn't want to be either really—just trying it on—though he says he finished up as a mountain guide!

Our kids come up with the most incredible ideas, don't they? Hardly surprising when they're given so many options to choose from these days. And that coupled with the pressure to obtain qualifications. It's not surprising that our discussions with them are likely to take us into much that is frankly unrealistic territory. But they need us to join in the explorations, nonetheless.

'If I give up Maths and French—the teachers are no good anyway—and take up Art, I could start painting pictures and sell them. Then I could use the money to go to Central America and write an illustrated book about Mayan civilisation. I've been interested in that ever since I saw that programme on the telly last week. And I'm OK at English 'cos I got a B in the last test. I expect you'd have to help me out with the plane fare, though. But I'll pay you back when the book's published!'

Let them explore. Don't just say it's a lot of rubbish. Encourage your children not to fall into the ruts set by society. Let them be adventurous in their ideas.

But we also have to challenge them. 'Um, sounds interesting. Tell you what, why not paint one or two pictures in your spare time and see how much money you get for them? And get a book from the library on the Mayans.'

Or to the would-be brain surgeon, 'Are you being realistic about this? Do you really want to spend seven years qualifying to be a doctor when you got minus fifteen in your last Maths exam and they kicked you out of the Biology class for 'liberating' all the white rats? And we're still paying for that explosion in the Chemistry lab. Are you sure this is your calling?'

At the end of the day the unpalatable truth is that qualifying for most jobs requires some sort of perseverance, be that in making applications, going for interviews, or obtaining academic qualifications. We have to ride with our kids, challenging, encouraging, until they can see for themselves what they really want to do—and what they in reality *could* do.

We were fascinated to see how Jesus 'powerboated' with his disciples when he fed the five thousand. The story is recorded in Matthew 14.

A great crowd had followed Jesus and spent the day listening to him. He appeared to be oblivious to their physical needs and come evening his responsible disciples in a show of maturity, just like our teenagers when they're hungry, suggested that as it was getting late he should dismiss the crowd so they could all get something to eat.

Jesus responded by giving them the opportunity to take the initiative. 'They do not need to go away, you give them something to eat.' Take the lead. Think out how you're going to do it.

That set them muttering among themselves. 'What have we got? Five measly loaves and two glorified fish fingers! You're joking. What's he expect us to do with that? How can we feed this lot with five loaves and two fish?' That's the point at which they faced reality.

Then Jesus stepped in, 'Bring them here to me. Direct

the people to sit down on the grass.' Ah, they can manage that.

He takes the bread and the fish, gives thanks and breaks the loaves. He's full of faith. One day they will be, but not yet.

It would be tempting at this point for Jesus, having shown up the immaturity of his disciples, to have carried on without their assistance. Imagine how they would have felt left standing idly by, trying to look cool in order to disguise their sense of inadequacy, while he got on with the job. Jesus was a better 'parent' than that. He involved them again. 'You go and give it to the people,' he said.

Yet Jesus didn't simply create a mountain of bread and fish for them to distribute. The disciples were intimately involved in the miraculous process. Somewhere between his hands giving to them and they to the crowds, the food multiplied. Instead of feeling foolish, they were privileged to take part in an amazing example of divine power.

When to challenge, when to help, when to entrust. That's powerboating wisdom!

If we would follow Jesus' example, then we will have to take some risks with our kids. Now it sounds very mature to say that you should give your children freedom commensurate with their sense of responsibility. But that idea is, in fact, unworkable. It leaves you in a dilemma: they're not very responsible, so I can't give them any more freedom; but if I don't give them more freedom, how will they learn to be responsible?

What we actually have to do is to increase their freedom beyond their responsibility, but in measured doses. In other words, we must allow them to make mistakes. Our job is to ensure that they don't have so much liberty that the mistake turns into an absolute disaster. The pattern is: risk, mistake or success, increased responsibility, risk again—and so on.

The best example we can think of is learning to drive a car. It's no use waiting until the pupil is 'responsible' before you risk venturing on to the roads, otherwise you'd spend the rest of your days parked in the driveway. Instead, the instructor/pupil relationship is one of 'controlled risk', with a view to progressively reducing the control until the pupil has full responsibility for the vehicle.

That's how people mature. Jesus understood it. 'One day,' he said to his disciples, 'you will do greater works than I do.'

A lifeboat

There are times when we have to change into lifeboats.

Mike and Jean's teenage son decided to run away from home. They were good parents, nothing awful had happened at home. But their son was going through a complicated time of life. He suddenly felt he wanted to be free, to escape.

The police found him eventually and phoned his parents. They drove down to fetch him. The story is repeated a thousand times over. How are they to respond to him?

It's tempting to be angry, or to lecture, or even to counsel. You enter the police station and say, 'Thank God we found you. We're so glad you're all right.' Then you get him in the car and it starts, 'You know your mum and I were very upset by you running off. It's been a nasty shock and your mum has had to go to the doctor because of her nerves. She's been given tranquillisers. And I've had to take time off work. And that's not easy for me at this time of year. For all that, we do forgive you but we think you ought to learn some lessons out of this. And we want to try to get to the bottom of why you did it.'

It's the wrong approach altogether. Your runaway kid is full to the throat with conflicting emotions. He's relieved, but sorry. He feels guilty, but a bit resentful. He's glad you came, but may well feel that you're the reason he went in the first place. And nothing has changed. He needs time and space to think, and a chance to say what he really feels.

It's better to do what the father did in the story of the prodigal son. Welcome your child back. Have a celebration because he's come home. Time for deep chats later—when he's ready for it.

Fortunately, most of our rescue operations will be less dramatic than this. The issues are far more likely to be matters such as getting refunds from shops, or asking a Year Head to change a wrongly-chosen study option. Or, of course, it may be because a friendship has broken down. On this, you may think they should never have entered the relationship in the first place, but that's not the point now. Your child is hurt, depressed and feeling lonely. Mum and Dad to the rescue!

When to be a lighthouse, or a powerboat, or a lifeboat needs wisdom. In other words, as the saying goes, it requires a flexible response to the situation. This is no time for us to get set in our ways. We have to fight the moral flab of middle years and keep at the spiritual aerobics. And you never know, we may even grow to like it!

4

Let's Be Friends

There are times when beacon-flashes of light illuminate our path for a brief instant and in those moments we see the otherwise hidden signpost which shows us the direction we should take. It's called revelation. Such was our experience when Debbie was approaching her teens. And on our signpost were written the words 'Become friends'.

At first we didn't altogether understand it. After all, we already loved our daughter and had a very happy relationship with her. Then we remembered the words of Jesus to his disciples, 'I no longer call you servants.... Instead, I have called you friends' (John 15:15). The change marked not only the growing confidence Jesus had in his disciples' grasp of truth but also his desire for an adult relationship with them. And, as the Master, it was his prerogative to initiate this.

We understood then that we must initiate a similar change in our relationship with our children. The Mum and Dad of childhood must become the friends of the emerging adult. But what did that involve?

Consult and confide

The first thing we discovered was that we had to command less and to consult more. When children are young, we tell them what to do and we expect them quite properly to obey us. If they refuse, we have various ways of enforcing our will over theirs. Successful parents ensure that Mum and Dad win on all the important matters. That's fine for children.

But it's not the way to treat friends. Start commanding your friends, with threats of sanctions if they don't obey, and they won't be your friends for long! Friendship is based upon goodwill, upon a freely-agreed consensus of ideas. Friends discuss and come to a mutual understanding, because that's what both parties want. They do what they agree is the best thing all round.

That's what it means to become friends with our children. We begin to treat them as adults and to take them into our confidence. When they ask, 'Why?' instead of replying, 'Because I say so,' we reason with them. (You may always have done this with them. The difference now is that you expect them to understand your reasons.) We explain our position. We ask what they think and take that into account in our decision making.

Another thing we do with our friends is to share our feelings with them. When children are young, it's inappropriate to unburden our hearts on to them. But as they move towards adulthood, it's a good and necessary thing to do.

We are not suggesting by this that they should be overloaded. After all, they still have a very limited experience of life. Certainly it is unwise to share, for example, marriage problems with young teens. Such matters require adult counsel. And if you're a single parent then be careful not to lay too much of the problems of loneliness on to your child because that may only increase the child's own sense of isolation. You need to talk to brothers and sisters in the church about those kinds of problems.

Having said that, most children respond very well when

we drop the parental masks and let them know how we really feel. It helps if you can say, 'Sorry, I'm feeling under the weather today,' or, 'We've just had a big bill and we're not sure at the moment if we can afford to pay it,' or, 'Actually, I'm feeling very hurt over what Auntie May said on the phone yesterday.'

Our children pray for us because they are aware of our feelings and we've made known to them what our needs are. In fact, we ask them to pray for us, and very often they gain a spiritual insight denied to us. Revelation does not come according to age!

Of course, this easy-going mutual friendship doesn't happen overnight. There are still times in early teens when Mum and Dad have to lay down the law. And children aren't always receptive to being treated as adult confidantes. It will take several years until, all being well, you have a full adult relationship with them. And you may not evolve out of having to dictate bedtimes and the acceptable state of their rooms until they are all of eighteen! The important thing is to observe the signpost and make the initial commitment to change.

Time and space

Let's be honest about it. If friendship is to happen we must give our teenagers time.

Sitting watching TV with them (the staple opiate of the masses) doesn't count, unless perhaps you use the time to discuss the values being communicated, or the programme serves as a means of giving the family a real laugh together.

We mean time when you can talk, when you can share, when you can grow to understand and appreciate one another.

It would be no exaggeration to say that we have felt on occasions that our children's whole future turned upon us being there at the right time. That only really happens if we are already committed to making them a genuine priority in our lives.

Unless we spend time 'by the wayside', playing sport, walking together, cooking together, visiting places, true friendship will never develop. It's no use sitting a child in an armchair and saying, 'We need to talk! Let's now talk!' Such an artificial approach to conversation is doomed from the start.

Real communication takes place not when we are 'working at our relationship' but as a by-product of some shared activity. The rise of so much counselling these days is a reflection on the loss of easy-going friendship where people shared their hearts and received advice without scarcely being aware that it was happening.

This kind of time is the most precious gift we can bestow on our children.

Letting off steam

Spending time with our children in a developing adult friendship will not necessarily be the easiest of matters. We knew a man once who complained that his biggest problem in this area was simply coping with the immature ideas and feelings of his young teenage daughter. How do you develop an intelligent relationship with a child who comes out with sentences like, 'I've decided I want to be a social worker and I want to live in a forest miles from anyone, 'cos I'm fed up with people!'

The secret is not to take such statements too seriously. If we wade in as parents with, 'Stop talking such nonsense, you silly child!' we'll soon put paid to friendship. Extreme ideas in teenagers simply reflect a lack of experience. Immaturity, as we keep emphasising, is not sin and therefore shouldn't be rebuked as though it was.

We might do well also to remember that the truth often lies at the extremes. The danger of being mature and 'balanced' is that, as with the mid-point of a see-saw, there's no movement at all. Our safe world may in fact be static and thus actually false to the truth about life. Teenagers often see that better than we do. Hence their willingness to experiment with ideas, be they ever so wild.

All children need the opportunity to let off steam, especially teenagers. Sooner or later they'll do it anyway, but when you sense a head of steam is building up, you might try this for an idea. Go for a walk with your child, or sit with him in his room, wherever he's relaxed, and say something like: 'Listen, Mike, I want you to feel free to say anything you like about anything you want. Blow your top if you want to! If you're fed up with me, if you're fed up with your mum, if you're fed up with your brothers and sisters, fed up with school or church, if you hate the pastor, then you can say so. Even if you feel like hating God, say so. I'm not going to condemn you, punish you, or correct you. Let rip and say what you like!'

You will probably never have rebellious teenagers if you provide them with such opportunities from time to time. Rebellion is born out of inner frustration. It comes from the feeling that one has no choice, no say in what is happening, or even the right to complain.

Just recently we encountered a sixteen-year-old boy who kept walking out of church in the middle of the meeting. It wasn't that he didn't wish to be there, simply that his parents gave him no choice. They failed to hear his feelings about the subject. If only they would say one Sunday morning, 'Why don't you stay in bed and give church a miss today?' He might actually do that for one Sunday, but he'd be back the next, by his own free choice. Instead, every Sunday he'd come along with all those bottled-up feelings and express them in the only way he knew how.

The Bible says, 'In your anger, do not sin' (Ephesians

4:26). To let our children get it all out of their system on occasions is not to make them sin. And in any case, if they do go a bit over the top, they'll be more aware of it than you. Leave them to sort it out with God. He has a good reputation for understanding. After all, he's coped with psalmists who came up with such edifying gems as, 'Break the teeth in their mouths, O God,' and, 'Happy shall he be who takes your little ones and dashes them against the rock!' Nothing if not an honest expression of how they felt!

Your children may want to be angry about hush-hush subjects in your church, like: 'If God's a God of love, why is there all this suffering in the world? Why isn't our church doing anything about Ethiopia? Why aren't the older folk as thrilled with Jesus as we are? Why are there people in our church who read the *Daily Express?* Why aren't we praying for Northern Ireland in our meetings? Why are all the deacons so old? And why is Mr Jones allowed to be one when he's so miserable?'

There have been many occasions when we have been quite sobered by allowing our children to be really honest with us; times when we have needed to repent; times when we have realised that we were blind. We parents need the humility to learn. It's tempting for us to feel our children are being unfair, unbalanced and unloving when they let rip. But just listen, and later meditate on what they've said. They might just have a point. And we may need to say sorry.

When it hurts

Friendship inevitably involves some hurts born out of misunderstanding, thoughtlessness and disagreement. In fact, the closer you get to somebody the higher the risk of this happening. This is why marriage is the most blessed of human relationships but at the same time also the hardest to succeed at. The mark of a healthy relationship is not that you never have problems but that you know how to resolve them.

We've already noted Ephesians 4:26. It says, 'In your anger, do not sin. Do not let the sun go down while you are still angry, and do not give the devil a foothold.'

Not letting the sun go down on our wrath is the secret. For husbands and wives it means never going to sleep with back-to-back fellowship. Never, ever! We think we can say with integrity, that in twenty-three years of marriage, we have never succeeded in going to sleep with an unresolved issue. Not that we haven't tried, of course!

It means we have been preserved from resentment and bitterness.

We must do the same with our teenagers. It's a bit harder with them because we no longer put them to bed, nor do we share the same room. It's much easier to have the row and simmer in front of the TV while they go to their room not to be seen until the next morning. We parents have to take the initiative in reconciliation. That's the responsibility of the stronger party.

It involves being the first to say sorry. The issue may not have been your fault, but the fact that it developed into a row is both your faults, so start the apologising. The word 'sorry' probably contains more power to win teenagers than any other in the English language.

At the end of the day it doesn't really matter whose fault it was. After all, we're not Trade Unionists trying to negotiate percentages. The important issue is that you and your child are out of fellowship. The goal is reconciliation before sundown. It's no use waiting until they come and say sorry. Why should they? They feel as hurt as you do. And you're the mature one! So you initiate it. That's the way to win your children's hearts.

Breaking the curse

We don't believe it's necessary for Christian children to be either wimps or rebels. It's perfectly possible to raise children with robust characters who will stick right with you throughout their teenage years. In fact, that is one of the promises of the gospel.

The last words of the last book in the Old Testament anticipate a day coming when parents and children will be reconciled.

> See, I will send you the prophet Elijah before that great and dreadful day of the Lord comes. He will turn the hearts of the fathers to their children, and the hearts of the children to their fathers; or else I will come and strike the land with a curse (Malachi 4:5–6).

Good relationships between parents and their teenagers are a prophetic mark of the New Covenant and a sign that the kingdom of God has come. In a nation which is so clearly under a curse for lack of this, there can scarce be a more important issue.

When most of us were teenagers there were the beginnings of what was called the 'Generation Gap'. A wedge was being driven between parents and children. Different values, different cultures, the breakdown of relationships. Home life began to disintegrate. Today it has reached crisis level with a vast number of broken homes and countless shattered relationships between parents and their children. The land is smitten with a curse and we must heal it.

That healing begins in our own homes. There is no point in preaching the gospel on street corners, attending prayer meetings and conferences, singing great songs and knowing all there is to know about the faith, if we aren't friends with our kids. This has to be the priority of our lives.

Some of us may feel we struggle with it, perhaps almost to the point of despair. Renew your faith! Pray that God will annul the curse in your family. Recognise what is going on in your children's lives. Be understanding. Get close to them, however inconvenient it seems at times. Show them that they are loved and accepted. Let them know that you want their friendship. And God will honour you.

Others of us are cut to the quick by all this. We know that we are seriously out of relationship with our children. The Holy Spirit is convicting us urgently that we should take the initiative in putting matters right. It's not easy, but it's essential that we reach out before it becomes too late. The barriers harden. Love can be lost for ever. Reaching out through our own pride and pain costs, but the price is worth it if it means reconciliation, forgiveness and healing all round.

Homework

We want to give you some homework. It's very simple; just ask each of your teenagers these three questions, and take note of the answers. We suggest each parent does this separately and then compares notes.

Question 1: What makes you happiest about me?
Question 2: What irritates you most about me?
Question 3: What would you most like to see improved or changed in our relationship?

It's important that you listen when you do this. Ask your children what they mean by their answers, if they're not clear, but don't disagree with them. This is their opportunity to say what they feel. You must not be defensive, otherwise they'll either clam up, or this constructive exercise will turn into a row.

Be grateful to God for what they like about you. Be sobered by what they don't like! And ask for their ideas about how you might together initiate some improvements in the relationship. You may be surprised at how good their suggestions are.

Part Two

Earrings, Walkmans and Levis

5

Where Cultures Clash

Someone once said that the secret of managing a hot potato is to keep it in the air most of the time!

That's perhaps how you'll feel about our approach to this next section, as we juggle with the conflict that arises between secular culture and our Christian counter-culture. For there are no easy answers to the problem of being in the world but not of the world, and even fewer when it comes to guiding our children through the maze of cultural options available to them today.

For many parents it's a potato that becomes too hot to handle and differences of opinion over such matters as music, clothes, reading material, television, alcohol and smoking become major sources of argument with their teenagers—so much so that these issues may undermine the whole relationship.

The reason for this is simple: culture is very personal. It affects our tastes, our values and beliefs, and our hopes and fears. So we feel strongly about the issue—especially when someone else's culture intrudes into our 'space', as for example when Madonna is blaring from your child's bedroom and your preference is for Dire Straits, or the Beatles, or even Beethoven!

Added to this, the conflict between Christianity and

secularism is a real one. The issue is more than one of taste. It's also to do with truth. The apostle John says, 'We know that we are children of God, and that the whole world is under the control of the evil one' (1 John 5:19). It's hardly surprising then that we should want to protect our children from 'the world'.

But we cannot withdraw from it. For one thing, we are called to be salt and light, and that means dwelling in the midst of society, just as Jesus did. Furthermore, we cannot say it's all bad. That would be to deny God's creation and his undoubted blessings even upon unbelieving mankind. Do you refuse to eat ice cream because it was invented by non-Christians? Or do you not shop in an arcade designed by pagan architects? We have to live in the real world as best we can. That means holding to what is good, refusing what is evil, and changing for the better what we can. It's a complex task and little wonder we sometimes get our fingers burnt when we try to get a grip on this particular potato!

Christians used to talk about 'worldliness', by which they meant the bad side of secular culture. But if we still use such a term, what do we mean by it? Is Brahms any less worldly than Bananarama? Are discos more worldly than jazz or folk clubs, or pubs than restaurants? Is 'toplessness' abroad more worldly than bikinis at home? Does Jackie Collins really write in a more worldly fashion than Agatha Christie?

Many parents would like simple yes/no answers to such matters. A published list of decrees from headquarters would solve the problem. Just look it up in the book. Prescribed music, fashions and reading matter for the year would surely make life easier.

Or would it? Like frankly isn't that simple. The plain fact of the matter is that the legalistic approach doesn't work. Not least because there are so many things the Bible doesn't pronounce upon. It's not possible, for example, to decree the biblical length of a skirt or whether studded leather jackets are in order. The moment we start attempting to produce our authorised lists on such matters we move away from revelation and on to personal opinion. Not surprisingly, our kids may feel every right to challenge our authority on the subject.

Instead, we must seek to understand and to apply the principles of God's word to our contemporary world. By thus becoming wise and discerning, we'll be able to show our children the timeless relevance of the Scriptures to the issues of their own lives and so teach them to live pure, free and fulfilled in Christ. We'll also greatly reduce the occasions for conflict between us and them. And that can't be bad!

However, before we explore this path, we must take note of the secular cultural terrain through which we are at present passing. It is surprisingly religious.

The cult of 'outerness'

Most of the culture which influences our teenagers comes from one common source—be it New York or New Orleans, London or Liverpool, modern culture originates in the city. Provincial towns and country villages, once strong sources of culture and community themselves, now bow to the all-prevailing influence of the city's style.

It is, in fact, a relatively small caucus of city-focused media people which influences the lives of millions of today's young people. Deeply committed to the same beliefs, promoting their own image and type, their ideas pour out endlessly through the television, the radio, newspapers and magazines. So much so that in spite of differences in children's personalities, there is today a veneer of cultural 'teenagerness' which is recognisably the same in almost any part of the nation.

It has produced what we choose to call the cult of 'outerness'—the adoption of images, fashions, lifestyles and values, not because these have been thought through by our kids, or even been handed down from previous generations, but simply because this is what the media decrees is 'in'.

Here's a trivial but typical example of what we mean in the realm of fashion. Levis have brought out jeans which have buttons instead of zips. Why? We aren't told. Years ago, buttons were superseded by the zip because the latter was more reliable and looked better. (It may present a threat to certain parts of the male anatomy but is considerably less embarrassing than the dreaded missing button!) Why return to a redundant technology? Because somebody has come up with the novel idea of doing so. A gimmick, no less, which the manufacturers hope will sell more of their product.

And no doubt it will, because the new style jeans are powerfully promoted as what every cool customer is wearing. Subliminal images of youthfulness, ego-enhancement and increased sexual attractiveness—underlying which is a value system quite unperceived by the average buyer—all serve to convince him that he must have this product.

The Levis advertising machine is only one aspect of the whole. People are constantly being persuaded to adopt the latest music or make-up, paperback morality or consumer novelty, without ever really understanding what's going on. Never before has a generation been so manipulated and conditioned by the mass-media as today. Yuppies, your world is ruled! And you know not by whom, or how or why!

At first sight this might seem harmless enough. After all, vulnerable as they are, most children don't grow up that bad. And it surely isn't wrong to wear Levis! But all the time there's a subtle conditioning taking place; a gentle, pleasurable urging to conform to the status quo of the image-makers. And beneath that lies something more sinister.

Imagine if you will the gods of this age. They are invisible. They have no shape or form. But they have their teachers, their evangelists and a multitude of worshippers enticed into service at an ever earlier age. They take the place of Christ.

We'll have a brief look at two of them.

Romanticism—the goddess of sex and violence

In 2 Samuel 13 we have recorded one of the most sordid stories in the Bible. It is the tale of Amnon and Tamar. The first verse sets the scene. 'In the course of time, Amnon son of David fell in love with Tamar, the beautiful sister of Absalom son of David.' Tamar was Amnon's half-sister. His love for her was incestuous.

Incestuous love is wrong. It is contrary to the will of God. Amnon knew it, as did everybody else in those days. The law of Moses was quite clear and they believed in the law of Moses. But Amnon fell in love with Tamar, and that feeling was allowed to override all other considerations until it became the one ruling passion in his life.

Driven by desire for the forbidden, he cruelly raped Tamar.

And then he hated her. His 'love' turned out to be a mirage, a self-deception to sophisticate a lust which once sated could no longer conceal its true identity. But the love/hate goddess was satisfied.

This wretched story contains all the essential elements of modern-day romanticism: feelings divorced from reality and truth; rebellion against what is right in the sight of God; the association of sex and violence.

Romanticism is one of the most pervasive philosophies of our generation; it is the supreme spiritual, creative and adventurous force in our teenage culture. Virtually all popular forms of art, music and literature reflect and proclaim its values. The strutting stars of pop lead the worship, popular porno authors write the devotional books, film-makers, photographers and artists provide the icons, TV personalities give their testimonies, 'experts' teach the doctrines. Multitudes follow, and the goddess is once again satisfied.

We see the fruits of this idolatry in teenage promiscuity, in sexual violence and perversion, in marital unfaithfulness, in addiction to pornographic literature, videos and films, in drug addiction, in rebellion against authority. But it goes deeper. Romanticism is a parody of the truth. It offers excitement, adventure, passion and creative fulfilment—all the things one gets with authentic Christianity—but through service to a false god.

Why children from Christian homes find all this so difficult to resist we'll see a little further on.

Sensualism—the god of self-indulgence

The second is perhaps a little more familiar. In Philippians 3:18–19 Paul says: 'For, as I have often told you before and now say again even with tears, many live as enemies of the cross of Christ. Their destiny is destruction, their god is their stomach, and their glory is in their shame. Their mind is on earthly things.'

This is what in *The Healthy Alternative*[1] John called 'the belly god'. It is that tendency of human nature towards sensual indulgence without any thanksgiving to God.

It is, of course, perfectly right and good to enjoy pleasurable sensations. God made us that way. He gave us skin that feels pleasant when it's stroked. He gave us appetites that can be satisfied with food and with drink, noses to enjoy smells, eyes to behold beauty. His one requirement was that we should render thanks and worship to him as his proper due and as our proper response.

So when, for example, we enjoy a meal, we should praise the Lord. And when a husband and wife make love together, they should do the same. A satisfying piece of music should evoke thanksgiving. Rather than denying pleasure, the Christian should actually get more pleasure out of life than the unbeliever. 1 Timothy 4:4–5 says, 'For everything God created is good, and nothing is to be rejected if it is received with thanksgiving, because it is consecrated by the word of God and prayer.'

However, for the sensualist the pleasures have become an end in themselves, pure self-indulgence. There is no thanksgiving to God, no glorifying of his name for these gifts, and no moderation of desires in accordance with the degree to which those thanks can be rendered. Appetite unlimited!

We see it so clearly in present-day consumerism. Why is it that our society demands an endless supply of consumer goods? Precisely because of the influence of this god.

Now, we're not suggesting for a moment that it's wrong to enjoy the benefits and comforts of modern technology—simply that we should beware of the deceitfulness of this god. Jesus said, 'Watch out! Be on your guard against all kinds of greed; a man's life does not consist in the abundance of his possessions' (Luke 12:15). There is a seductiveness in all this. Like the foolish husband intoxicated by an illicit affair, we lose sight of reality, we persuade ourselves that we need this, it's all right, we're still in control.

Falling into debt is only one symptom of losing control. There are others far worse.

Why is it that advertisers and promoters invest such enormous amounts of energy, time and money to convince us that what Jesus said isn't true? Simply because they themselves are trapped in the same circle of sensual greed.

They too want to be able to indulge their appetites in the service of this god.

Teenagers are bored because they are being conned! The belly god never satisfies. However much is received, self-gratification cannot give meaning or purpose to life. It can only make you feel good at the most superficial of levels. And after a while that becomes boring, if not downright irritating.

We've got to help our children see through the lies and myths of modern society. Romanticism and sensualism are false gods. Neither we nor they must bow down and worship them.

Note

[1] John Houghton, *The Healthy Alternative* (Kingsway: Eastbourne, 1985).

6

Reaction or Revelation?

Start talking to teenagers about culture and they quickly become edgy. What do you know about it? Are you trying to impose your antiquated values on us? The world's moved on since you were young! Leave us alone to make up our own minds.

And they are partly right. We do react from our own prejudices. Here's an example of what we mean. John's mum never used make-up. I rarely use any. He says I'm too beautiful to need it, in any case! So he was quite convinced that his daughters never were going to paint their faces, let alone wear earrings when they became teenagers. Very biblical, very sound was my husband; a man of the word—not a man of the world!

Then our daughters reached those fascinating years. Guess what they wanted? And forcibly so. To give John credit, he did a humble re-examination of his views. Was he really being biblical or was he merely prejudiced by his own upbringing, or for that matter by his personal preferences?

The result? Our beautiful daughters wear earrings and make-up!

Often we don't immediately know why we react. Some things just feel wrong. In the late sixties we used to call it 'bad vibrations'. It isn't an explanation that will satisfy today's questing children, who view such ideas of their parents as incredibly naïve. Rationalism once more rules!

Sometimes our reaction is based purely upon a mistrust of the unfamiliar—in other words, it's a subtle form of fear. At other times it may be because, say, the music just isn't to our taste. It's perfectly valid to feel like this and it helps our kids if they can understand that it's our problem, not theirs. Trouble brews when we allow our personal reactions to be projected as though it was all their fault. That's when they feel got at.

There's a world of difference between, 'That's terrible music,' meaning, 'I don't like it,' and, 'That's terrible music,' meaning, 'You've got lousy taste,' or, 'It is evil music and you shouldn't be listening to it.' We must know the difference, and so must our children.

Of course, there are many occasions when we may be genuinely discerning something evil—the spirit of the age, romanticism or sensualism. That form of reaction is justified and we must seek to teach our children how to recognise this.

A paraphrased version of 1 John 2:15–17 may read: 'Do not love secular society or anything in secular society. If anyone loves secular society the love of the Father is not in him. For everything in this secular society—the lusts of the flesh, the lust of his eyes and the boasting of what he has done and does—comes not from the Father but from secular society. Secular society and its desires pass away, but the man who does the will of God lives for ever.'

Pretty strong stuff. And even more so in Revelation 18 where the code word 'Babylon' represents a society, its commerce and culture, passing away under the judgement of God. Little wonder then that we should react when we perceive the same spirit in our own age. It's right to do so.

But when we do, let's make sure we are aware of the real issues.

The heart of the matter

The prophet Isaiah seemed at one point to take quite a detailed interest in women's clothing.

> The Lord says, "The women of Zion are haughty, walking along with outstretched necks, flirting with their eyes, tripping along with mincing steps, with ornaments jingling on their ankles. Therefore the Lord will bring sores on the heads of the women of Zion; the Lord will make their scalps bald." In that day the Lord will snatch away their finery: the bangles and headbands and crescent necklaces, the ear-rings and bracelets and veils, the head-dresses and ankle chains and sashes, the perfume bottles and charms, the signet rings and nose rings, the fine robes and the capes and cloaks, the purses and mirrors, and the linen garments and tiaras and shawls (Isaiah 3:16–23).

What does it mean? Why is God suddenly against necklaces, bracelets and perfume? Many times the church has read passages like this and failed to get the real point. Instead, decrees have been issued forbidding women to dress in anything other than drab. The dowdier you are the holier you must be!

But that isn't what Isaiah is getting at. He is opposed, not to the jewellery, but to the heart attitude which it manifested in his day. The context is one of a socially and economically divided nation. The prophet attacks the outward manifestation of the luxury-loving, arrogant, glamorous rich as his way of revealing the truth about their hearts.

The issue then is not one of whether it is right or wrong to wear earrings but of whether the wearing of such is part of a callous indifference to the plight of the poor. That message is tremendously relevant in a day when it is so easy to purchase yet another piece of expensive fashion without even giving a consideration as to whether the money should be put to the benefit of someone else in need.

Here's another illustration of the importance of heart attitudes: 'You have spent enough time in the past doing what pagans choose to do—living in debauchery, lust, drunkenness, orgies, carousing and detestable idolatry' (1 Peter 4:3).

The Christians in Peter's day were prepared to be thought strange because they forsook the party-loving, drunken, orgiastic, drug-taking culture that they had been part of. It was for them an issue of discipleship.

Peter's words continue to have relevance, especially to certain kinds of discos which our children may be invited to attend. It's legitimate to ask a Christian in such an environment, 'What's a nice girl [or guy] like you doing in a place like this?' But it doesn't follow that our children should be banned from attending all discos or parties, or that they should be forbidden ever to listen to pop music. Living under grace requires that we assess each disco on its moral merits, rather than simply issuing blanket decrees from the aloofness of our armchairs.

There are Christians who feel that the only way to cope with all this is to withdraw completely. They become exclusive brethren, or enter monasteries, or become ascetics in the hills and deserts where separation from the world means living with only the most basic necessities of food, clothing and shelter.

Not that this is the answer. The story is told of a Christian hermit who was tempted by a band of demons. They tried everything they could to make him sin—storms, heat, lustful visions, promises of wealth—all to no avail, for the man had truly separated himself from the world and its comforts. Then one day the devil himself was passing by. The demons in desperation sought his advice. With a sly wink, the devil approached the hermit and whispered these words in his ear: 'Your brother has just been made Bishop of Constantinople.' It worked with fiendish success. At once, the hermit was filled with jealousy. Separate from society he was, but he could not separate himself from his own heart.

Evangelicals, by and large, do not choose the path of asceticism because of their clear responsibility to witness for Christ in the midst of the everyday world. The trouble is, and our teenagers see this more clearly than we do, instead of retreating into the desert, we often retreat into the past. We kid ourselves that history sanctifies culture. Hence, the music of Beethoven, Tchaikovsky and Chopin is treated as more acceptable than that of say David Bowie, Elton John or Boy George.

Yet society was as sinful then as today. Tchaikovsky was gay, Brahms a dirty old man. Chopin's *Magic Flute* is based upon the rites of Freemasonry. Even John Dowland's lute music was considered riotous in its time.

Or, to come more up-to-date, do you recall the years of Rock 'n' Roll? Wonderful stuff! The music of our teens. But our parents didn't think so. They were still into the dance bands of the forties and when the now tame film *Rock Around the Clock* hit the screen they thought, quite rightly in fact, that a revolution had just begun.

The Beatles' song *Yellow Submarine* is now sung as a nursery rhyme in our primary schools. Made safe by the years. Yet it was, when released, a song used to promote the drug culture.

The same phenomenon happens in the world of fashion. Take jeans again—though we're not obsessed with the topic! A revolution took place in women's jeans in the early sixties. Until then most wore a side zip variety. Then came raunchy front zip jeans for women, liberating and sexy. Christian women of the time had real problems with the fashion and the image associated with it. But not any longer. Time has sanctified jeans. The same goes for trouser suits, bikinis and so forth. Not for nothing are evangelicals called conservative! Nor is it surprising that our teenagers consider us always old-fashioned and reactionary.

Yet up to a point putting the clock back works. Cultural spirits do lose their power over the years. What causes sin in one generation may not do so a generation later.

The reason for this is quite simple: the spirits behind the cultural icons of our society are only sustained by men's worship. While a demon has worshippers the idol will have power. Once replaced by something else, it loses that power and becomes simply 'nice'. Hence Satan, 'the Prince of this world', seeks continually to capture the hearts of each new generation with some novel attraction. It worries him little that the power to corrupt may be short-lived, provided he can keep the process going—and he has a pretty impressive track record so far!

It is, to our minds, a pity that Christians have not been equally zealous in producing a culture with sufficient vibrancy to seriously challenge Satan's sway. Most of what the church has come up with is either born out of a ghetto mentality or is merely a morally sterilised version of what the world does better in the first place. But how to remedy this dismal state of affairs is beyond the scope of this book. Anxious parents want to know how to guide and protect their children through the temptations of the world that now is. Even so, it's high time the gauntlet was thrown down.

Merely reacting superficially against the world leaves us in the not very inspiring position of having to refuse almost everything fashionable and to live instead with Satan's cultural cast-offs. There is a better way.

True Christian discernment is concerned with the effect of things on the heart. Does my listening to this music, visiting this place, reading this book, draw me nearer to God or drive a wedge between us? Am I uplifted or depressed by the thing I give myself to? Am I provoked to give thanks or made to sin?

But Christian discernment is also concerned with what we transmit by our behaviour. As we've seen, it's tempting for parents to retreat into the past. That tells the world that our gospel has no relevance for today. It also makes our kids feel the odd ones out among their peers for all the wrong reasons.

We would like to suggest that a better approach is to take the world as we find it, a mixture of good and bad, and use its resources so that we might become a revelation of the good news in the way that we express our culture. We'll take fashion and music as two ways of illustrating how we, and our teenagers, can do this.

7

Dress to Bless

Clothes can be a real area of conflict in teenage years. How can our children be an authentic revelation of Christ in the way that they dress?

Speaking of the behaviour of wives in regard to their husbands, even those disobedient to the word, Peter writes, 'Your beauty should not come from outward adornment, such as braided hair and the wearing of gold jewellery and fine clothes. Instead, it should be that of your inner self, the unfading beauty of a gentle and quiet spirit, which is of great worth in God's sight' (1 Peter 3:3–4).

Paul writes to Timothy in a similar vein: 'I also want women to dress modestly, with decency and propriety, not with braided hair or gold or pearls or expensive clothes, but with good deeds, appropriate for women who profess to worship God' (1 Timothy 2:9–10).

These two passages have often been interpreted in a manner which suggests that female spirituality is best demonstrated by dowdiness. If you look attractive you must be unspiritual! The old Authorised Version translation didn't help by translating the word 'decency' as 'shamefacedness'. Hardly surprising that the world should look at some Christian women and say, 'What a shame!'

The original Greek actually carries a different meaning.

It suggests that God wants you to be tidy and harmonious. He wants your clothing to be measured by good values and by what is appropriate to the situation. A woman's inner beauty in Christ should be allowed to shine forth in the way that she dresses, so that she becomes a walking revelation of the gospel. This doesn't mean wearing T-shirts covered in texts or jackets bestrewn with badges! We're talking about the outward expression of inner values, not the religious *Yellow Pages* on legs!

Clearly the flashy glamour of the *Dynasty* or *Dallas* clothes-horses is inappropriate for Christians. And it is obviously unbecoming for a Christian woman to dress like a woman of the streets. But it is equally a bad witness for her to dress scruffily.

Jan feels strongly that mums should be good examples for their daughters to follow. They should never feel ashamed of how we look, either because we're such a frightful mess or because we look like mutton dressed up as lamb. Young-looking fashions are one thing, but teenage clothes seldom go well with thirty-five-year-old faces and hips! We should look after ourselves, care for our hair, feel comfortable and at ease because we dress to suit the occasion. It doesn't take a lot of money to do so, just a sense of self-worth. And it's that which our children need to learn from us.

Teenagers need to be aware that there are modes of dress which express something quite contrary to the gospel. Blatant seductiveness is one of these. Particularly at party times we should encourage our girls to check on the message their clothes might be transmitting.

Another current anti-gospel fashion is Goth, the tendency to dress in drab black. Goth philosophy is obsessed with death and alienation. Christians are gripped by life! We are accepted in Christ and full of hope. Funeral shrouds do not become us.

Aside from the veto against men dressing up as women (or vice versa) recorded in Deuteronomy 22:5, the Bible has little to say about men's fashion. This may mean we shouldn't say too much, either! However, clothes are to do with image and image is a communication of what we are, or what we want people to think we are. And that's where radical Christian values come in.

So we may legitimately question whether our sons should opt for, say, the Rambo style of clothing which suggests violence and revenge. Similarly, bovver boots and shorn heads, or studded leather and chains convey a message of anger against society. Male earrings have associations with romanticism and homosexuality in particular. It's right that as parents we should discuss with our sons whether these are the images they really want to communicate or whether they've just got caught up in a current trend.

Sometimes maintaining a Christian value system does set us visibly apart from those around us. That can be difficult for a young teenager and we must be sensitive to the fact. We do our boys no favours if, for example, we insist that dressing as a Christian means wearing a scaled-down version of Dad's clothes. There's no reason why a Christian lad shouldn't look 'cool' and dress with style.

Fortunately, at the present time there is no difficulty in obtaining fashionable clothes which our sons can wear with pride to express manly Christian virtues. Let's encourage them to do so.

One way of seeking to become a revelation of Christ in our clothing is to be guided by the fruit of the Spirit. For instance, a girl may decide, 'Well, today I'm going to dress to demonstrate the peace [or joy] of God.' 'This week I want to communicate the love of God in the way that I clothe myself.' 'My style will be restrained today because

I'm going to show the self-control of the Holy Spirit in my life.'

In other words we should try to communicate some of the values of who we are. It's helpful to look at yourself and ask, 'What comes through of my character today?' We may find that we have styles for long seasons which express the dominant characteristics of God's work in us. You may have a child that is naturally very joyful and flamboyant. Well, that can be the joy of the Holy Spirit. They may love to dress in bright colours. That's not contrary to the word of God. That is expressing the joy of God.

Be ready for anything. Your child might just turn up looking like a rainbow, with the defence that they're only reflecting God's covenant today!

Approaching the subject this way is far better than just conforming to the in fashions of the media-manipulated world—let alone falling for the New Age legalism of personal colour coding and the like. Let's encourage our children to discover what best expresses themselves in Christ.

To do this they will need freedom to experiment, as well as good advice. Letting them know when they've got it right is far more constructive than criticising them when they make a mistake. Many a foolish parent has ruined a child's day by telling them they look awful just as they're leaving the front door and it's too late to do anything about it. We can all afford to live for a while with garish hairstyles and make-up experiments which didn't quite come off. It's part of the fun of growing up.

And let them be a revelation of themselves in Christ, not of you. We must allow our teenagers the room to find and express their own Christian identity. They have different faces to you, they have different characters. And, remember, they're of a different age!

8

The Singer and the Song

Here's another subject fraught with potential for domestic nuclear escalation. Music makes the heart glad; it can also drive the parents mad!

Music is one of the most powerfully uniting forces in the world. For that reason, it is also one of the most divisive. Attack teenagers' musical tastes and you attack their culture and their generation. For it is the medium through which they express their ideas and values—just as we did in our own youth. You may wonder how, but their music gives them comfort and security. Woe to you if you seek to disturb it!

But disturb it you will, if only to avoid your eardrums rupturing. High volume seems to be part of the very nature of some pop music. It doesn't really work if it's played quietly. At least, that's what they tell you! Nevertheless, you have a reasonable case to insist that you shouldn't have to listen to their music if you don't want to, any more than they should be obliged to listen to yours.

Decibel levels can be controlled by regular reminders—and there's always the headphones if everything else fails (though it's worth pointing out that listening to music through earphones at high volume can permanently impair your child's hearing).

The kind of music they listen to is another matter altogether and one which needs to be handled with wisdom.

Many Christian parents have serious misgivings about the whole pop scene. This isn't helped by stories of the Lord's Prayer being recited backwards by so-called satanic groups, and the like. (Believe it corrupts if you want to, but it seems to us that to say things backwards is childish rather than sinister. There are more subtle dangers elsewhere.)

It's easy to denounce the whole scene, switch on the latest *Spring-Hosanna-Downs-Royal-Restored-New-Harvest-Frontier-Festival-Bible Week* worship tape, and insist that's all there is to it. None of this promiscuous rock rubbish! Songs of Zion alone shall grace our ears in this home!

Musical taste is highly subjective. It is also age-sensitive. However much we try, most of us will still find ourselves more at home with the music of our own youth than with the music our children now listen to. That in itself is enough reason for us to avoid over-hasty judgements on their preferences. Here are a few other factors to take into consideration before we pull the plug on their ghetto-blasters.

Music and moods

The impact of a piece of music is strongly conditioned by the environment in which it's played. For example, you might consider a piece of march music to be good listening. And so it may be, until it's used by an Adolf Hitler to stir up his fanatics at a Nazi rally. Immediately, the music takes on sinister connotations.

Or you may hear what to you is a perfectly awful jangle, only to find that the same music expresses perfectly the anguish you feel when the newscasters report an awful atrocity somewhere in the world.

Images and associations change the feel of music. Ravel's *Bolero* is a passionate composition in its own right but few would have viewed it as music for making love to, until it was used that way in the widely-watched film *10*.

It isn't then possible morally to categorise music apart from the culture and usage of that music. And, as we saw with *Yellow Submarine,* that usage may change from heavy drug scene to nursery class over a period of time.

It's a point worth making to our kids. 'Wot's wrong wiv listening to *Bend My Mind, Bend My Body?* I fink it's good music,' may need the reply, 'Perhaps. But would you really want to sit down and listen to a group of gays trying to get you to join them, if they were just talking and not singing?' One of the great powers of music is its ability to draw us in. The Pied Piper still plays his tune. He may lead children to the mouth of the pit. Some fall in.

If music can carry a message because of its associations, if can also reinforce or change the mood we are in. 'Listen, they're playing our tune, darling!' is a reminder of the happy days of our courtship. By the same token a piece of music may recall a painful, broken relationship. Kids can easily associate particular tracks and albums with good times or bad times in their experience and use that music either to reflect what they feel or to change their present feelings.

Natural Noises

James 1:17 says, 'Every good and perfect gift is from above, coming down from the Father of heavenly lights, who does not change like shifting shadows.' One of the implications of this text is that there is no such thing as a holy musical style as such. All melody, rhythm and harmony is from God. It's how these are put together and used by man which has the potential for good or evil.

It's no surprise then to find that many of the modern worship songs which bless people across the world have rock rhythms. Lots are written by musicians whose styles were formed by the Beatles era. Yet those same rhythms can be used to promote sex and violence.

Many Christians would like to believe that there is a 'natural' (by which they mean sweet and quiet) type of music in the created world. When we moved to our new house, we were treated to the full repertoire of a song thrush every day, beginning at about three o'clock in the morning. The music was lovely, the programme timing appalling!

But God has other kinds of music in creation. He has his own heavy metal sounds when he slams the senses with a veritable well of sound that drowns out all other perceptions. The Niagara Falls has that effect, so does a full-blooded July thunderstorm over the South Downs. The Bible says the sound of the saints when they're worshipping is like the sound of many waters, like the roar, the overwhelming ear-blasting, mind-numbing thunder of a gigantic waterfall—heavy metal, if you like.

God has his rhythms in nature. He has his howls. You may say of the wind, 'Ah, the gentle breeze of God's music.' But have you ever listened to a winter gale? Howling, whistling, weird, macabre—it's all part of God's creation, because God is a God of infinite variety.

Different music, like the varying moods of nature, blesses in different ways at different times. John finds it very difficult to work with earphones on and rock music pounding in the middle of his brain. It doesn't help his sermon preparation! But there are times when he has sat in traffic jams in the centre of London and turned Radio One up full blast, and that has brought peace and order into his life. It's his way of fighting back against the discordant jangle of city traffic. Our children do their homework quite happily with the same music. It's their way of fighting back against the discordant jangle of their overstretched brains!

Lyrics and lifestyles

Ah, but what about the words? Some are quite disgusting, others promote rebellion and anger. Most are fairly neutral and simply reflect a modern teenager's view of the world around. These lyrics are helpful because they are assisting our children to articulate what they really feel about life. That may not be what we would like them to feel, but it may have a lot more reality than our ideal, orthodox Christianity.

Of course, a good deal of the time they're not really listening to the words, anyway. That can be a safety factor; it can also lead to a subtle indoctrination. We must teach our children to be aware of what they're listening to. Certainly we should encourage them to avoid profane lyrics and those which put destructive moods into their souls.

The vulnerable are most at risk. Those without values, or those in rebellion against your values, can be affected. But kids with otherwise well-balanced lives will see most rock music as just entertainment, or even education as to what their peers are thinking. After all, it's worth remembering that acid rock did not lead most of us into the drug culture in the early seventies any more than most of us become Freemasons by listening to *Magic Flute*. We are convinced that, evil as the world is, God and his providential goodness is far more powerful.

If we sometimes have problems with types of music, we may also find that the lifestyles of many composers and performers aren't to our taste, either. Up to a point that no more disqualifies a piece of good music than the lifestyle of your milkman disqualifies the milk he delivers. Sinners are quite capable of drawing on God's providential goodness.

The difference between the music and a bottle of milk, however, is that milk merely nourishes our bodies. Music affects our personalities and our values. And modern rock cannot be divorced entirely from the lifestyle of the performer and indeed the visual imagery which goes with the rock video.

It is a fact that much modern music is blatant propaganda for immoral and dissolute living, often exemplified in the performer's own lifestyle. Young and impressionable teenagers, caught up with the excitement of life, are easily conditioned into accepting anti-Christian values. Rock music can be very sensual; it fits well with a promiscuous age, and it'll do our children no harm to be aware of that fact.

Music, like wallpaper, is subjective. It's to do with the effect that it has on us. And that provides a key to assessing the rightness or otherwise of a piece of music. Can you give thanks to God for it? 1 Timothy 4:4 says: 'Everything created by God is good, and nothing is to be rejected if it is received with thanksgiving, because it is consecrated by the word of God and prayer.'

If our children can honestly thank God for their music, it's OK—at least for them. We may not be able to do the same ourselves. That's fine. All it then needs is a little mutual understanding about volume controls!

9

Discernment

The sea of history is littered with islands once inhabited by those who thought it possible for Christians to live entirely separate from the surrounding waters of secular culture. Each in its turn has been deserted and all that remains are ruined edifices and follies. That same sea is also littered with the corpses and wrecks of those who drifted unthinkingly with the tide of public opinion; a tide which seduced them fatally on to quicksands, treacherous reefs and the cruel coastlines of spiritual compromise.

But dotted here and there are fine craft in full sail. These boats are driven by the fair breeze of the Spirit. Their masters steer a skilful course with the confidence born of good instruction and learned experience, for they know the whereabouts of the deep water channels, and how to avoid the rocks and treacherous tides.

It's possible to isolate ourselves from the world; it's very easy to drift unthinkingly with the tide of popular opinion. But God wants us to do neither. Faced with the challenge of our culture he wants us instead to exercise true spiritual discernment; in other words, we must learn how to distinguish good from evil. Hebrews 5:14 tells us that this is the mark of the mature person—hence, a worthy goal for us parents!

Discernment develops as we learn how to apply the Scriptures to the issues which confront our daily lives. This is of particular importance when it comes to facing those subjects and situations upon which the Bible does not pronounce specifically. That's when we need to have a good grasp of spiritual principles.

Here are one or two examples of what we mean. In Philippians 4:8 Paul writes, 'Whatever is pure, whatever is lovely, whatever is admirable...think about such things.'

That's helpful advice in an age of cynicism. Today's teenagers are led to doubt whether there's anything truly good. It's fashionable to attack 'nice' things. Satire of the *Spitting Image* type is very popular. Attractive monuments are defaced with aerosol graffiti. Sick humour, sordid tit-bits and tales of violence constitute much popular reading matter and locker-room conversation.

This emphasis on baseness lowers people's self-esteem. It discourages aspiration and instead fosters failure, mediocrity and indifference. You don't have to be a very acute observer of the British way of life to see that this is a national disease.

Anyone can knock down the achievements of the past; few people can re-create them. Virtue is easier criticised than copied. Those who wish to build their lives successfully will fail in the attempt if they only study the demolition jobs on others.

We must help our children to see through this prevailing mentality; they must discern these negative attitudes for what they are—and reject them in favour of something better. Teach your children that goodness is 'cool'. Encourage them to nobler values than those of their non-Christian friends around them. Help them to appreciate good things and not to be afraid to have genuine heroes and personal aspirations.

Another helpful principle for discernment is found in 1

Corinthians 6:12. Here Paul is dealing with a catch-phrase which was doing the rounds. 'I'm old enough to do what I like. There's no harm in it. Everything is permissible to me.' The apostle nods sagely and replies, 'Sure. But not everything's beneficial, is it?'

He goes further. 'Everything's permissible to me; but I won't allow myself to be mastered by anything.' This is a useful argument when it comes to, say, smoking or other drug-taking. Nowhere does the Bible condemn cigarettes as such, so it is quite permissible for Christians to smoke and still go to heaven. (You might get there a bit quicker, actually!) But it most certainly isn't beneficial. It masters you. So the Christian says, 'I could do it, but I choose not to, because it is unhelpful and I'm not going to let anything like that take away my freedom.'

Paul applies this principle in the realm of sexual morality. People were saying, 'The stomach's for food, and food for the stomach. You feel like sex—have it.' But God never intended that the body should be used for immorality. To do so is to abuse God's purpose. Therefore, it's unacceptable for Christians to be immoral. It's a bit like using a telephone handset as a hammer. Something gets broken.

Is it all right for a Christian to go to the disco? Nowhere does the Bible say, 'Thou shalt not go to the disco!' But will that particular disco be beneficial; will it enhance your freedom in Christ and enable you to keep your body for the use God intended, or otherwise? Let them judge it for themselves.

What kind of magazines and books should they read? Where do they go on holiday, and who with? The same principle of discernment applies.

What should they do about alcohol? There are many Christians today who feel it's appropriate and part of their freedom in Christ to drink moderate amounts of alcohol.

There are many for whom that would be deadly dangerous. Our children have got to find out for themselves what is freedom for their lives, and what is bondage. We must not lay upon them a legalistic anti-drinking attitude or a legalistic drinking attitude. They must discern for themselves. It is, after all, just as legalistic to say, 'Thou shalt drink,' as to say, 'Thou shalt not drink.'

Christian discernment challenges the roots of both religious legalism and the permissive bondage of the secular world. It is based upon grace, but not cheap grace. What we are suggesting isn't a licence for our kids to do as they please, but a way of giving them a real strength and responsibility when it comes to taking on the pressures of the world around them. It's teaching their eyes to see.

This all takes time, and we may have to be patient while they work it out. We have met Christian punks with bright orange Mohican haircuts, half a dozen earrings in their ears, pins stuck through their noses, dressed all in black, pounding their brains out with heavy rock. Now, we don't think they yet understand how to manifest the Spirit of Christ through their lifestyle. They have adopted something else for want of discerning anything better. They're God's confused childlren, but the confusions pass and sooner or later they begin, in most cases, to see that the only really radical way of life is to be a disciple of Jesus Christ.

Pray we must, worry we will, attack we mustn't. Confrontation does have its place, but far less so than we think. There are often wiser ways of correcting their extremes.

Many years ago, we had a phase in our then church for hot pants. John never spoke from the pulpit to condemn it. Instead, we encouraged folk to joke about it. The result? The girls who were participating in the craze saw the funny side of it, realised it was a somewhat inappropriate fashion for church, and dropped it. If John had ranted from the pulpit about provocative thighs, it would probably have provoked the wrong reaction. The girls would either have stopped coming or have felt they had to score a point. For to be sure, they were not deliberately dressing to seduce the deacons! A breath of gentle humour often has more power than a fierce trumpet blast.

So, these things need sensitive handling. Do let them have some fun. Great powers may operate behind society, but our children are better insulated than we think. Let's not drive them into extremes of over-reaction or self-rejection by condemning everything they try. Instead, let's encourage them to live by grace and so discover with thankfulness all the good gifts of God which will make their lives worth living to the full.

Homework

What irritates or worries you about your child's lifestyle? Talk it through with your teenager as one who wishes to learn how he ticks. Don't confront him, but enquire.

Ask your child to imagine he is you. Would he approve or disapprove of the things that worry you? Ask him why and seek to learn from his answers something of the way in which he sees things.

Part Three

Love, Sex and Mirages

10

The Mother of Harlots

We cannot avoid her; this gross, scarlet Mother of Harlots, presiding with cynical lust over the affairs of men. Babylon the Great. City without Shame. The whole earth is polluted with her blasphemies and adulteries!

Today, with the explosion of information technology there is no escape from this Babylonian culture which we call 'the world'. Newspapers, magazines, videos, radio and television ensure the encounter takes place, not in pagan temples but in the sanctity of our own homes. The choice is plain: let Babylon into your lives or lose touch with what is happening in the real world. Only those who wish totally to withdraw can hope to remain unaffected by its all-pervasive influence.

But escapism is not a valid option for our teenage children—or for us parents. So we must take on the world. And in no area of life is the ensuing conflict of values more real than in the realm of sexual beliefs and practices.

For the past three decades, the Mother of Harlots has revelled in promoting the indulgence of everything that is sexually perverse and decadent. As a result, we raise our children in a society which is sexually more confused than probably any previous generation.

Are they homosexual or heterosexual, or something in between? Should they sleep around? Do condoms really protect you from AIDS? Who wants 'safe sex', anyway? Masturbation is good for you, but pornography is sexist. Unless you're a woman—then female erotica is liberating! But what's the difference? Sex before marriage is essential to finding out if you are compatible. But why marry? Unwanted babies can be killed before they're born, but child abusers should be brought to justice. Why this inconsistency?

John expressed something of the current confusion in a recent poem.

Ah, little girl so sweet,
Play innocent in the street,
You'll grow up soon.
And then they'll teach you what to do.

Who are you?
A female form
Designed for men;
But why?
A woman's touch is far more kind.

Let us open up your mind,
Explore the taboos of the past;
Be not afraid;
For God is dead.
At last!

And your friend,
The little boy.
He'll grow up, too.
Confused.
Uncertain who he is;
He must not be a chauvinist!

Perhaps he's gay?
Many are;
Or so they say.

Find out;
Come out; cry out.
The church won't mind;
They rather like the other kind!

But hedge your bets,
You might be straight.
Just as well to copulate
With those of other sex than you.

Leisure, pleasure,
Lots of fun;
Sex is good for anyone.
Condoms keep you safe from AIDS,
And all the other nasty things
That give promiscuous sex a sting.

At least,
That's what the experts say;
And no one's taught
A better way!

It's tempting to press the panic button at this point. How are our children to cope with all this? What can we do to protect them? It appears a daunting task and one from which we may well wish to flee.

But better to face the foe than to pretend the foe doesn't exist. And that, sadly, is the trouble with many Christian parents. Sex is a taboo subject, a constant source of embarrassment to them. So much so that some are too embarrassed even to admit that they are embarrassed! It's an attitude which is of no help to our children. Ostriches may know a lot about sand but they are poor guides for crossing the desert.

John was approached at a teenagers' conference by a young man with this typical cry. He said, 'I'm in a terrible mess. If you saw me at home I'm a good Christian boy, but on the inside I'm a sex maniac. But I can't talk to my parents about it.'

There was nothing abnormal about this lad. He certainly wasn't a sex maniac! But he was wrestling with normal teenage desires in a world which had plunged him into a personal battle between his Christian beliefs and the provocation of Babylon. He felt ill-equipped to fight it. The real tragedy was his inability to communicate the problem to his parents—and that was mostly their fault.

This embarrassed silence, this implication that sex is impolite and unclean, can have devastating effects. The young woman from a good Christian home may optimistically enter upon marriage only to find that she is sexually frigid because of an unconscious shame engendered by her parents' negative attitudes. It could ruin the marriage.

The opposite can also happen. A church leader's daughter gets pregnant by her boyfriend. Why? Because she rebelled against her parents' prudery and lack of understanding. Or a son becomes a libertine at college because he doesn't want the patently inhibited sex-life he perceives his parents to have.

However difficult we may find it, we must face the issues square on with our kids. They need intelligent guidance from us if they are to find their way through the sexual minefield.

Secular society has been far from afraid to talk about the subject. Books, television documentaries, sex education lessons, magazines, all ensure that no aspect of human sexual behaviour is left untouched. As a result, our children probably know more than we do about 'the facts of life'.

Unfortunately, what the world does so well, it also does so unrighteously. Sex is taught as something you do when you fancy it, like eating ice cream or going to the pictures. Most modern sex education is divorced from Christian ideas of chastity, covenant love and marital faithfulness.

Technique has replaced trust, contraception is more important than commitment, satisfying the libido substitutes for sustaining love.

And this is no accident. Those who influence the ideas and practices of men and women in society have quite deliberately rejected the Christian way. In fact, most sex education today is based upon the assumption that the church (and therefore God) is the cause of all the trouble in the past and true liberation is found by positively rejecting its standards.

Root of rebellion

All modern secular sexual values have sprung from a root of rebellion against the will of God. This is especially true concerning the ideas of chastity before marriage and of faithfulness within marriage.

Four ideas have been used to make this rebellion sound intelligent and advanced. It'll help us in guiding our children if we know a little bit about them.

God messes you up

In the late fifties and early sixties the ideas of the psychologist Sigmund Freud became popular.

The root cause of much of the stress in our lives is due to an unhealthy restraint on our latent sexual desires. This is brought about by a repressive conscience called the 'superego'. It was created by the taboos imposed on us as children by our parents, society and the church. This superego is in direct conflict with our libido, or primeval sex drive. The result is inner tension which expresses itself in neurotic behaviour.

The average reader may be forgiven for concluding from this that too much self-restraint is supposed to send you barmy!

Freud had a point, of course. A society in which people

are not allowed to express their emotions or to talk about their deep feelings will produce some very uptight individuals. But it is quite another thing to imply that chastity, self-control and fidelity are a sign of being sexually neurotic. The virtues have become overnight the vices and vice versa!

The proposed remedy for all this was to throw off the restraints of the superego and thus give vent to all our basic animal desires. Hence, it is now healthy to masturbate, to sleep together out of wedlock, and to lust after your neighbour's partner. Purity is sick, and so are those who teach it!

We once had in our church a woman who attempted suicide. Fortunately, we were able to save her life, but the hospital put her under a psychiatrist. He counselled her thus: 'The reason you attempted suicide, the cause of all your problems, is your church and your religion. What you need to do is stop attending these church meetings, go down the pub, pick up a bloke or two, get laid a few times and you'll feel much better.' Pure popular Freudianism! Thankfully the girl in question refused the counsel and sought God instead.

Monkey business

There was a time when, if we wanted to understand mankind, we looked to the best we had produced. We studied the lives of saints and heroes, of great thinkers and leaders. It was their characters which challenged and inspired us to attain our full humanity. But that's all changed. Nowadays, we go instead to London Zoo and watch the behaviour of the chimpanzees at their tea party.

Once we believed we were made in the image of God; now we are merely monkeys who have evolved out of their fur. Instead of looking up for inspiration we look down for explanation. The body language of apes, especially their rituals of courtship and copulation, debunks all the mystery and magic of human love. Morality is a myth, religion a rip-off. Primates of the world unite—you have nothing to lose but your souls!

It's not true, of course. Fortunately, God keeps enough artists, poets and saints in the world to remind us otherwise. But the pervasive myth has been used to justify the morals of alley-cats among those first created in the image of God.

Apparently, we can do as we please. Since animals cannot be held morally responsible, any kind of sexual behaviour is permissible. In this human zoo men are supposed always to be randy and women permanently on heat. Like animals, they may play the courtship ritual and copulate all they like, when and with whom they like.

The resultant anguish is appalling; guilt, pain, confusion, shame, use and abuse, mistrust and hatred. 'Why, O why do I feel like this if I'm only a naked ape?' We've had a society that's tried to live like animals and then found they got hurt like humans.

Rock on, baby!

In a previous section we took a brief look at romanticism, that philosophy which is at once exciting and adventurous but seeks the thrills of life in the forbidden, the perverse and the rebellious.

Lady Chatterley's Lover opened the avenue for exploring these realms in popular literature. Rock music has played a significant part in directing juvenile eroticism along the same paths rather than those of sexual fulfilment in marriage. Rock music isn't wrong, nor for that matter is eroticism. It's the ends to which they are presently directed which cause all the problems.

Because music is so much a part of our teenage culture, the sexual message is easily received. Until Christians gain a greater influence in the rock industry, romanticism will hold sway, immorality will continue to be glorified in passionate song, and multitudes of young people will keep up the pretence that it's great. Make no mistake, romanticism's false fires of love and sacrifice but thinly conceal the ashes of lust and death.

Love is all you need

The fourth factor is a semi-religious one. Remember the Beatles' song *All You Need Is Love*? That song popularised a theology which went something like this: in the past we had rigid laws dictating our conduct. Today we have the option of total licence—do as you please. But that is obviously fraught with difficulties. Is there another way, some middle ground, something we can cling to in the absence of any absolute standards?

The answer was apparently to be found in the Bible—'Love is the fulfilment of the law' (Romans 13:10). All you need is love. Provided what you do is loving, then you don't have to worry about any absolute laws. Love preserves you from going down the path of total licence and at the same time gives you the flexibility to meet any situation without recourse to rigid rules.

It sounds very fine at first sight. But if we set love over against absolute standards, we finish up making God's commands the enemies of true love. Instead of love being the correct heart attitude with which to fulfil the law it fast becomes the alternative to law—a lawless love, no less!

In fact, what happened was that the *feeling* of love became an absolute law in its own right. Hence, when parents complained of their children's immoral behaviour they were met with the apparently unarguable response, 'But we're in love!'

When the noble, sacrificial love of God is reduced to the pleasure principle, anything goes. In the French pornographic novel, *L'Histoire d'O,* the central character is abused in every manner conceivable and accepts it all willingly—because *l'amour,* 'love', is absolute. Even sexual violence becomes defensible with the plaintive cry, 'But I love you!'

When these four ideas first came on the scene, people believed that sex was the greatest thing on earth. It was love. Today's young people are still taught this, but cynicism is setting in. They're not finding the permissive path all it's cracked up to be. In fact, it's proving to be full of pitfalls and potholes. Since the advent of AIDS you can even die from sex!

The sex act has become for many a charade, a pretence at enjoyment, something that everyone is expected to do during their teens. Gone is even the thrill of rebellion.

One of the sad effects of all this is that it is now estimated that some thirty per cent of young people who get married stop having sexual relationships within six to nine months of marriage. Thinking they've found love through sex, they enter marriage on that basis, only to find that this isn't the way life works. Boredom, disappointment, disillusionment—people give up on it.

That, of course, creates tremendous tensions and pressures in the marriage. The disappointed are always tempted to see if the grass is greener on the other side of the fence. Abstinence is fertile soil for adultery.

It has to be said that some kind of rebellion in the realm of sex was justified. The world of the forties and fifties was repressed and legalistic in many ways. Typical of the attitudes was a Christian book which did the rounds in our teenages years and which warned of the sins of young men wearing bathing trunks on the beach and exposing their bare chests. The veto was enforced—it has to be said, dishonestly—with dire warnings of skin cancer to those who insisted on persisting with this flagrant display of flesh. Goodness knows what the author would have made of today's topless fashions!

More seriously, a lot of people suffered needless

anguish and heartache because of the prevailing hush-hush attitudes. Those who needed help couldn't get it. Frustration was rife, ignorance commonplace. But what was needed was not a rebellion against morality but a revolution into God's true freedom. The latter has been a long time coming.

11

Practise What You Preach

There is an important prophecy in Jeremiah 31:29 concerning the Incarnation and the coming of the kingdom of God. 'In those days people will no longer say, "The fathers have eaten sour grapes, and the children's teeth are set on edge."'

A time is coming when people will take responsibility for their own sins, says Jeremiah. No longer will they excuse themselves by blaming their parents. Indeed, a New Covenant will be formed, and the people of that covenant will delight in heart obedience to God's laws.

The prophecy offers great hope for us anxious parents. Why should our teenagers and young adults have their teeth set on edge any longer because of the sexual sour grapes eaten by the previous generation? It is surely time for the people of the New Covenant to set about rearing a generation for whom love and sex are sweet and beautiful, and where bitterness in relationships becomes a thing of the past.

Whether this happens or not will depend to a large extent upon us. We want to suggest that there are three things that we can do to help our children make a success of their sex lives.

Keep your own house in order

No man is an island. 'Free love' is very costly—and not just to the participants. The sins of the fathers (and mothers) are visited upon their children. Painful it may be, unfair it may seem, but that's one of the realities of life.

The first step in helping our children live sexually pure lives is that we do so ourselves. We must practise what we preach.

Past sins need resolving. You may yourself have been immoral. Hopefully, you have repented of the deeds, but sexual sins have a habit of lasting long in the memory. Feelings of guilt may arise every time we recall the acts of which we are now ashamed. If only we could start again! But it's too late. What's done is done. And we may fear that, in spite of all our efforts, the same things will happen to our children.

The gospel never minimises sin, or its consequences. But it does provide a remedy which is totally effective. The blood of Jesus cleanses us from all unrighteousness, and that includes sexual transgression. Jesus deals with both the guilt and the feelings of uncleanness which accompany sin. Sobered by our past we may be, but there is no need for us to wallow for ever in our shame. Rather, we ought to glory in the redeeming power of the cross of our Lord Jesus Christ.

True repentance is always worth it! Not only is it the key to saving our own souls but it contains the power to break the curse on our families. Iniquity doesn't have to pass from one generation to another, for God shows mercy to the thousands who love him. Part of what it means to be a new creation in Christ Jesus is to give your family a fresh start, free from the consequences of past sins.

If the past is taken care of, what of the present? The church is tragically littered with wrecked marriages because good Spirit-filled Christians somehow think they're immune from all sexual temptations and find to their cost that they're not. They fall into sin. Take care, for 'if you think you are standing firm, be careful that you don't fall!' (1 Corinthians 10:12).

Check...

...that you are free from adultery, and if you are a single parent, from the temptation to satisfy loneliness by lust. Coveting another person's partner still causes more marital break-up than any other single issue.

...that your heart is clear with regard to homosexuality. In spite of the fudging of the issue by some church leaders and the blatant defence of the practice by the 'gay Christian' lobby, the Scriptures make it quite plain that the practising homosexual does not have eternal life, any more than does the practising thief, liar or adulterer.

...that you have dealt with the issue of pornography and lustful masturbation. Jesus said that if your eye or hand causes you to sin then you should deal drastically with it. Better that than go to hell! (Matthew 5:27–30).

...that you have faced the issue of incest squarely. There is nothing more damaging to a child than to have been party to an incestuous relationship with a father or mother. It constitutes one of the most fundamental betrayals of trust in human relationships. Be on your guard against temptation, especially as your children enter their adolescent years.

Those are the negatives and it is a sad commentary on the state of the church that we find it necessary to write thus, but hard experience has taught us the need to do so.

Let your love shine

Now to something positive! The greatest help we can be to our children lies in us providing a role model of what loving relationships are all about. It's not enough that we tell our kids, 'Mummy and Daddy love each other.' They must see it demonstrated.

Love is a learned experience. It can't be taught from a book. Life-experience teaches children if they are loved or not. It also instructs them as to whether their parents really love one another.

Many children worry about this, particularly in a society where marital breakdown is rife. Rows between parents, simmering tensions and the like, hint that the family may be destroyed. And with that goes the child's own sense of security.

We are being watched! Teenage years especially are a time of acute observation. Our children will be profoundly affected by what they see and hear and feel. They need first-hand experience of that parental role model which we call 'a passionate covenant'.

True marriage is, after all, not just a piece of paper. It is a bonding of hearts and lives in passionate love to the extent that two people can call themselves one flesh for life. The will of God is nothing less, and that's what our children must see if they're going to believe that Christian marriage works.

Part of what this means is that parents should not be secretive or embarrassed about the sexual side of their relationship. We're not implying that you should embarrass your children by doing things in front of them that properly belong in the bedroom. But, they need to know that you make love and enjoy it—and there are plenty of signs of physical affection which can be shared in their presence, all of which say without words that love is real and love lasts.

In a healthy family children are secure in the aura of the love which their parents have for each other. And this is not simply an ethereal, spiritual love but one which permeates right down to the essential earthiness of the marriage bed.

Teenagers get to know if you are sexually satisfied. Acutely aware of the subject these days, they sense signs of frigidity or frustration. This doesn't mean you have to come down to breakfast with your arms around each other, saying in a loud voice, 'Wow, didn't we have a great time in bed last night, darling? Isn't it wonderful that we came to an orgasm at the same time—just like we always do?' Enough to make your kids choke on their cornflakes!

If it's going well, you won't need to say so. And if things could be improved, why not read our book *A Touch of Love*[1] for a complete guide to sexual fulfilment in the will of God? Even if you've been married for a number of years it can bring great refreshment to the relationship.

Make the subject open season

This is the third thing that we can do. Sex education should have commenced from the very first time they asked questions about where babies come from. With our own children we told them everything in blow by blow detail. It bored them silly! They were not the least bit interested and usually started playing with their toys after about two minutes. Fascination came later!

We thought it was better to tell them the truth when they were young rather than make up gooseberry bush stories which we would have to undo at a future date. Growing up with a knowledge of the subject which was as natural as anything else in life, there have never been really embarrassing moments, nor have we had to cope with the disinformation given out by schools. We got in first.

Even so, as children reach their teens, earlier with girls, there comes the time for that much-dreaded talk about the birds and the bees. Of course, if the subject is already familiar it will not be too embarrassing. Even so, expect some difficulty. Children at this age are self-conscious themselves. Their bodies are changing, as are their feelings also. The moment needs choosing with wisdom.

We suggest getting outside somewhere. Go for a walk. Holidays are a good time. Begin the conversation casually, something along these lines: 'Hey, son, you're looking good these days. Guess it's time we chatted a bit about growing up.'

By and large, mothers find it easier to talk to their daughters than fathers do to their sons. This is because mothers usually have the practical issue of periods to start the talk off. Fathers don't have that in the same way. They may be needing instead to talk about nocturnal emissions and masturbation. These are more difficult subjects to open up on. But it must be done. We owe it to our sons. Far better we talk openly than simply sling a book at them saying, 'Read that! Talk to me if you have any questions.' Because they won't.

If you're a single parent, you may be feeling cheesed off by now, because we're writing about Mums and Dads, and you're just feeling the pain of your own situation. What are you to do?

A single woman can obviously talk to her own daughters, but what about if she has sons? They need to hear from a man, and this is where the church comes in. The point of having brothers in Christ is not that they become substitute sexless husbands, but that as real brothers they help in the areas which need a man's input. Choose someone who is securely married, whose wife you get on well with, and who has a rapport with your son. Best if he has sons of his own. If you've got no one else, then talk to the youth leader, minister or elder. Ask, 'Will you chat with my son, please? To be honest I can't handle it and somebody needs to.'

Having opened the subject up, we've got to keep it open. One talk doesn't do it all. That doesn't mean becoming obsessive about it, but as children progress through their teenage years, their perceptions and needs change. We must respond intelligently and sensitively to them. There are several ways in which we can do this.

Note

[1] John and Janet Houghton, *A Touch of Love* (Kingsway: Eastbourne, 1986).

12

Keep Sex on the Agenda

Keeping the subject of sex and sexuality open means taking advantage of the natural opportunities that arise.

Body beautiful

For example, it's important that we acknowledge our children's maturing bodies and flatter them on their physical development. By this we mean expressing a genuine appreciation of their emerging adult figures. Needless to say, though the subject has its humorous side, we should avoid any kind of crudity—there's enough of that going around in the world as it is. We should also refrain from embarrassing our children in front of others. Most kids do not appreciate being greeted by Aunt Ethel with the words, 'Ooh, hasn't he *grown*!'

We all worry about how we look, and never more so than in those uncertain teenage years. Our task is to encourage self-confidence in our children. Better that Dad assures his daughter of her emerging beauty than for her to have to wait until she is desperate for a fellow to do so at any price.

Now, there obviously comes a time when girls need somebody else other than their fathers to tell them they're lovely, but if you have reassured them with cuddles and kind words that they are wanted and loved, when they do enter a relationship with a fellow it will be because they really want to, not because they are driven by insecurity and the need for physical acceptance.

One of the real problems we face today is the fact that girls in particular are being bombarded by the media with a message which tells them they do not look good. The not very subtle way this is done is by confronting them with ultra-glamorous models and pop stars who, for an absolute fortune spent on clothes, body shops, make-up and diets, can appear like goddesses.

The aim is to make your daughter feel ugly by comparison, unless—and here's the point—unless she spends a similar small fortune attempting to look like the model. No wonder many girls just have to buy new clothes every week and that their rooms are littered with hardly used make-ups, hair dyes and fashion flops. The fact that this hasn't happened to the same degree with fellows is simply because the media hasn't worked so thoroughly on male style.

Tell your daughter she does look all right. God didn't get the plans screwed up when he made her. Things may look too big, too small, too long, too short, too fat, too thin, but that's not the issue. God made her like that and somebody's going to love her the way she is. Out there, somewhere, is a fellow who's tuned to just her shape. Never mind if she responds with: 'Good grief, if he's looking for this shape, what kind of shape is *he* going to be in?'

Boys need equal encouragement. They want their muscles admired. 'Feel that bicep, Dad. Go on. It's harder than yours.' (It probably is.) They want to know that you appreciate their manly chests and the hairs growing on their legs—and, of course, the carefully cultured adolescent moustache. You'll have to get used to regular arm-wrestling as well. Sooner or later he will beat you at it—he's determined to try, anyway. Even Mum will have to go through the charade of taking on young Mr Universe.

Style is 'in' for boys. They want to look cool, not scruffy. What Mum thinks matters, because she is first representative of the female sex. If she's not impressed, will the girl down the road be? Boys want Mum's opinion and her encouragement.

The question of homosexuality

This seems a good point to pass some comment on the issue of homosexuality. It's certainly a subject which will be discussed at school and we will be wise to talk about it in the home.

Recent years have seen a concerted challenge mounted against the traditional Christian view which says that homosexuality is a perversion of God's intentions. Today it is being justified in schools and in the media as a valid option for young men. Even the AIDS crisis, which was introduced into Western society largely because of homosexual practices, has not deterred those who would push for positive discrimination in favour of homosexual orientation.

Recent legislation has helped curb this to some degree, but it is an unavoidable issue for our children. Because of the confusion and undoubted threat, we want to suggest how to protect our kids from within.

Straightaway, we must say that there is no real evidence to suggest that homosexual orientation is genetic. Children aren't 'born that way'. That is not to deny that we all have hereditary traits. Clearly we do. And one of these may be a certain effeminacy. However, though the girlish young man may find himself a particular target for homosexual attention, it is a fallacy to equate effeminacy with homosexuality.

The main factor which influences a child towards a sexual preference for his own kind is the lack of a proper parental role model. Hence, 'inner protection' for our children depends upon getting this right.

For example, one classic syndrome for inducing homosexual desires is that of the dominant mother and weak father. In a home where a bossy woman rules the roost while the father refuses to accept his God-given headship role, a young boy soon learns that women are a threat to his own male identity. He has only to observe the emasculation of his brow-beaten father, constantly harassed and in retreat, to be left with the increasing suspicion that women can hurt him, too.

He observes the emotional blackmail, experiences the histrionics, notes the lack of physical affection. As he grows up, he reacts. He may respond aggressively and become chauvinistic, even violent towards women. He may choose relationships with weak women in order to dominate them. Or, he may feel so utterly inadequate to form a relationship with a woman, that he turns to the company of men for his sexual satisfaction.

How important it is to observe and implement God's order for husband/wife relationships in the family. How essential for our children to see us demonstrating our affection for one another. It's here, above all, that they learn the naturalness, the beauty and the fun, the security and fulfilment of heterosexual love.

The other common factor in producing homosexual orientation is the absence, or inadequate provision, of a father. Deprivation of fatherly attention is always a bad thing for children. It is particularly bad for boys during the period of life around puberty onset and for a year or two beyond.

At this time, a natural process occurs for which we have recoined the term 'homophilia'—love of the same. It is manifested in the child developing an affection for his or her own sex, though the child would not recognise this as sexual and nor is it appropriate to credit such an embryonic phase with overt sexual desire.

The dynamics are very simple: the child is evolving into a sexually-aware adolescent. The release of hormones, the physical changes, force the child to find a new identity.

Psychological identity does not come about in a vacuum. It is largely formed out of relationships with others. Hence, during that insecure phase the child will look initially to those of the same kind as himself—one reason why hero worship is so common at this age. The hero may be a pop star, a teacher, a youth leader—best of all the child's father. If he is there.

In a healthy family, the homophilia stage will be handled by a wise father. A secure son will express considerable affection, and indeed physical affection, for his father at this age. This may appear to the father to contain a sexual element, which can be disturbing. But all that is happening is that the child is discovering what it feels like to be a man. He is irradiating himself with adult masculinity. In a very short while the process will be completed and the adolescent boy will emerge as a fully-fledged heterosexual. He may then turn his attentions briefly to his mother before looking outwards to the lush plains of girls unlimited!

This is a vulnerable time of life. Fathers and mothers in their turn, while responding to their child's need for more than usual, quasi-sexual attention, must beware of falling in to any kind of incest. Sadly, this happens all too often in our decadent society. Similarly, established homosexuals may take advantage of the child and draw him into sexual activity. Either way, the results will be nigh on disastrous.

There is another very evil possibility. It is that those with sinister motives may take advantage of this phase and teach that a child who feels an affinity for the same sex should consider himself homosexually orientated, at the least bi-sexual, and therefore free to engage in homosexual activity. The pubescent child, knowing that these feelings are taking place and not being given any other explanation for them, is then faced with the possibility of being 'gay'.

This knowledge can be traumatic in the extreme. Guilt, shame and self-revulsion on the one hand; ruinous homosexual experimentation on the other. All based upon a falsehood. Little wonder Jesus said, 'Woe to those who cause these young ones to stumble.' What should be an emergence into sexual security becomes a permanent identity crisis.

Dad needs to be around. The father always away on business, too tired to talk and irritated by his son's demand for physical attention when he is there, does a grave disservice to his offspring.

Our children's well-being is more important than our jobs, our church activities, our leisure interests. If we do not sacrifice our convenience we may well sacrifice their entire lives. Manliness is propagated by our presence; it is communicated by our gestures and our speech, it is observed in our activities. Our boys find their masculinity in the intimacy of our aura. No one else should be considered good enough to provide this, and we betray our sons if we ourselves fail to do so.

There is another major area in which fathers are absent today. It is in the single-parent family where Mum has the custody of the children and Dad is either dead or otherwise gone from the scene. We are painfully aware of the ache which this produces in the hearts of these mothers. 'Where am I going to find the man who can be the role model for my son. Will he be at the mercy of the unscrupulous? Will he never find his sexuality?'

This is a genuine problem. Many from single-parent

families do grow up sexually confused. It is one of the tragedies of a permissive society. However, there is real hope and it is to be found in the body of Christ, provided we rise to the challenge. God sets the solitary in families (Psalm 68:6). It is our conviction that as a practical expression of our true faith, every single-parent family should know a measure of adoption into a two-parent family in our churches. That this should be done voluntarily and with real pastoral wisdom goes without saying, but it is an effective way of facing the reality of the lack of a parent and goes some way to compensate for it.

Children without a father still need fathering. If the way isn't open for a younger widow or divorcee to remarry, then brothers in Christ need, in all purity, to go some way to fulfilling that adult role model.

It does not follow from all this that children from a dominant mother/weak father family, or children with an absent father, are automatically going to grow up homosexually inclined, any more than everyone catches a flu virus when it is doing the rounds. Life is more complex than that and there are many random factors which come into the picture. But just as we can take measures to greatly reduce the likelihood of us catching the flu, so we can take steps to provide our children with the emotional and spiritual health they need in these morally infectious days.

Confident virgins

Another way of keeping sexuality on the family agenda is to pick up on the attitudes that are going around the school, college or workplace. Sex is a regular topic of conversation, not always of polite conversation, in the world. Ask your children what their friends think about homosexuality, or divorce—or virginity.

It's quite possible that your child is the only self-confessed virgin in the class. (There will be others but they'll never dare admit it.) It can be a lonely role! Ask them how they cope. It will provide you with the opportunity to boost their confidence.

In times past, virginity was prized because it meant that a woman wasn't pregnant with someone else's child when she got married. In recent years virginity became a teenage complaint akin to acne—something you wanted to get rid of as soon as possible. But things are changing.

Encourage your kids that nowadays virginity is something to be prized again. It is no cause for shame. To be a virgin (male or female) means you are, to all intents and purposes, guaranteed free from syphilis, gonorrhoea, genital herpes, non-specific urethritis, genital warts, crab lice—and AIDS. It's not in fact true that everybody is at risk from the latter. If your kids are virgins and they marry virgins, they are practically immune from the AIDS epidemic. The only people at real risk from this disease are the promiscuous and drug abusers. (In this country blood products are now screened to make transmission by transfusion unlikely. There is some risk to those involved in the medical and associated professions.)

There are plenty of other good reasons for remaining a virgin until you are married, of course. Better a new car than a much-used old banger, and so forth! Build up your children's confidence. Chastity makes sense. Sleeping around is stupid.

Masturbation

Secular wisdom has reacted against the heavy condemnations and hypocrisies of the past by saying that masturbation is not only permissible but thoroughly good for you. We parents need to get our own thinking straight if we are to help our children in this vexed area.

Nowhere in the Bible does it say that the practice is

sinful. What it does condemn is the sin of lust. If masturbation takes place with lust, and realistically it often does, then the combination is wrong in the sight of God.

But we must be careful when we talk about this subject not to make our kids feel that even lustful masturbation is the worst sin under the sun. It's not! People are far more likely to go to hell for respectable sins like pride, self-righteousness, slander and envy than ever they are for masturbation. At least this practice tends to make folk feel rotten, with the potential for repentance, which is more than can generally be said for the others.

The subject needs sensitive handling. Angry confrontation is not the answer. By and large, they should be taught that it is an unhelpful practice to indulge in. Self-control is a better way. Give them practical advice about avoiding situations when they might be particularly vulnerable. This may be along the lines of not lying in bed for all of Saturday mornings, or spending too long in the loo. Your advice needs to include other ways of dealing with depression than by resorting to self-comfort. For boys in particular (both girls and boys are encouraged to masturbate these days) using up their excess energy in sports activity is an important aspect of sexual self-rule.

Take the opportunity to discuss pornography with your children. What's wrong with pornography? It debases women (and men too in hard porn). It treats women as less than human. It turns real people into two-dimensional fantasy images, reducing them to mere sex objects.

God made women in his image. There is, therefore, in every woman that which is Godlike. Pornography reduces people to the level of animal functions. It debases the noble image of God.

You may come across a pornographic magazine under your son's bed, or an erotic novel in your daughter's bag. You might even come in unexpectedly one evening to find your children watching a steamy 18-rated video. What are you going to do about it?

Wild outbursts seldom do any good. The fact that the item was hidden in the first place suggests that they already feel a certain sense of guilt. To come in heavy may only increase that to the point where in self-defence they argue a case which they don't really believe in. Most porn is viewed initially either out of curiosity (and let's face it, we are all insatiably curious about sex) or momentary weakness.

It requires quiet, rational discussion, encouragement to remain pure, and a clear reaffirmation of your wish not to have this stuff in the house. You can help them burn or otherwise dispose of the offending material.

Perhaps we should add here that our own reading and viewing habits should set a good example. Check your bookshelves. Are you happy that your children should read any and all of your books? Is your newspaper more to do with page-three boobs than world events? What do they find you watching on TV?

Having said all this, we must still avoid unreality. We do no favours to our children if we refuse to acknowledge the presence of lust in this world, or if we are unwilling to discuss sexual matters with them in a very down-to-earth and explicit manner. And much modern literature, for example, is not sexually exploitive but nevertheless explores frankly the sexual complexities and realities of human relationships. It may be perfectly legitimate for your children to study such literature for their GCSE examinations.

There's another point to be made, too. There is a world of difference between lustful looks and 'girl-watching', or for that matter 'boy-watching'. A lot of Christian men in particular have been in false bondage over this, feeling that to notice a pretty girl is to immediately fall into the sin of lust.

Yet God made her attractive, so why not notice her and give thanks to the Lord? Of course, we can be tempted to lust and that must be resisted. Some women go out of their way to be noticed in a purely sexual manner, but a studied look at their faces is usually enough to dispel lustful desires!

At a more prosaic level, your young teenagers will look at the opposite sex. Boys will sometimes spend time sitting on fences just looking at girls. Meanwhile, girls will sit in the intimate confines of the cafe glancing at and giggling together over some hunk waiting in the checkout queue. And why not? If our children never get to notice the opposite sex, they'll never marry! We must not rear them to think that they can only glance surreptitiously out of the corner of their eyes in the hope that you haven't noticed. God created the opposite sex. His word speaks unashamedly about human beauty and sexual attraction. It also warns about the sin of lust. Our job is to teach our children how, in the words of Paul, to: 'Test everything. Hold on to the good. Avoid every kind of evil' (1 Thessalonians 5:21–22).

13

Going Together

The first distant peals of wedding bells are sounding in our household as we write. Our eldest daughter has just become engaged to a fine young man. They are both believers, very much in love and seem well suited for each other. We feel our prayers have been answered.

Things have so far gone well for our Debbie, but we're well aware that they might not have. The Christian world is littered with the wrecks of ruined courtships and even broken marriages. There exists great confusion over boy/girl relationships in the church at large, far more so than in the world. Young people's fellowships regularly self-destruct because of fickle relationships, sexual competitiveness and the broken-heartedness that ensues. What can we do about it? What advice shall we give to our children?

The Christian problem ultimately revolves around one issue: we believe sex belongs only within the bounds of marriage. The non-Christian, on the other hand, believes that sex is for when you feel you are ready for it—and that is probably long before marriage. Hence, most unbelievers have no real moral qualms about exploring relationships sexually outside of wedlock.

This means that most relationships among unbelievers involve heavy petting early on, and in many cases intercourse at the first opportunity—the classic one-night stand is still the Saturday night goal for many young people. *Liaison sans lendemain* the French call it—a relationship without tomorrow. Very sad, when you think about it.

Serious relationships among non-Christians almost always include sex before marriage (if marriage takes place at all). It's worth noting that the world has replaced the specific, real promises of the marriage covenant with the undefined phrase 'we are committed' in order to justify their sinful practices.

When Christians go out together, because of their desire to obey God and not have intercourse outside of wedlock, they must play things much cooler. It is after all abject folly to stoke up the fire only to pour a bucket of cold water over it just as it's getting cosy!

There are really only two choices. Either we must go for totally chaperoned relationships—hardly workable these days—or we must exercise some form of self-chaperoning. In which case we need some guidelines which we can pass on to our children. You may find our own approach helpful. It goes something like this.

Volume control or graphic equaliser?

Most non-Christian relationships resemble the volume control on your stereo. You switch on and straightaway turn up the volume fairly loud—petting is soon pretty heavy. Before long it's full volume and the couple are having intercourse.

Many Christian young people adopt the same approach, except that they start the volume lower and don't want it to reach full volume until they are married. The trouble is, just when you think you've got it right, somebody walks by with a ghetto blaster blaring out and your volume seems far too tame by comparison. So you turn it up a bit.

Then your ears get adjusted to the new noise level, and soon it goes up a bit more. Before you know it, you are engaged in quite heavy petting and may find yourselves on the brink of having intercourse—the very thing you set out not to do.

The volume control approach to going together is too relative and undefined. It provides insufficient guidelines. A better approach is to plan your relationship to resemble the bands of a graphic equaliser.

As you probably know, the graphic equaliser is a means of splitting the tone control into several adjustable frequency bands. Each control covers a different range. Let's imagine that our graphic equaliser resembles five different levels of relationship, each one of them having sufficient range to allow a relationship to grow until, and if, you move on to the next one.

Band one—fellowship

A church shouldn't be run as though it were a nunnery or a monastery. It's healthy for teenage boys and girls to meet so that they can worship, serve and play as a group. We need YPFs where there's lots going on, not just Sunday morning Bible studies and religious events, but plenty of activities where they can enjoy being friends together.

To our mind it's unfair and unhelpful of parents to keep their children in a church where there are no other teenagers. It may be fine for the parents, but the children are being denied Christian fellowship among their peers. At the end of the day they may, in the absence of anything better being provided, opt for the world and in the process lose their faith.

In this 'fellowship band' let's encourage the value of singleness. The Bible has quite a lot to say about it. For instance, in 1 Corinthians 7:32–34, Paul says,

> I would like you to be free from concern. An unmarried man

> is concerned about the Lord's affairs—how he can please the Lord. But a married man is concerned about the affairs of this world—how he can please his wife [pay the bills, manage the kids, comfort her, etc]—and his interests are divided. An unmarried woman or virgin is concerned about the Lord's affairs: Her aim is to be devoted to the Lord in both body and spirit. But a married woman is concerned about the affairs of this world—how she can please her husband [wash his socks, cook him a meal, make the beds, etc].

What Paul is saying is that there is a calling in life called singleness. Unmarried teenagers are in that calling, at least for the present. There is no need for it to be a time of frustration or of disappointment. It can be, instead, a period of life during which we have undivided and totally fulfilled interests in the Lord. Let's scotch the myth that the only way you can find true happiness in life is with somebody of the opposite sex. It's just not true.

Jesus proved that you can have an absolutely fulfilled life as a single person. The apostle Paul elected, probably as a widower, to remain single for Jesus. Many very fulfilled young people take the same line. Chastity is good. Serving God with all this energy you have, including the sexual energy, is a great way of life. It doesn't need the complication of short-lived and often hurtful courtships.

Band two—special friends

One of the great merits of belonging to a Christian group is that you get the opportunity to know people at leisure and in a social context without any pressure to get closer. At least it should be that way in a healthy church. If everyone who walks in is automatically paired off by the rest, then much of that fellowship will be lost.

We say that because the next band of relationship is to do with forming a special friendship with someone of the opposite sex. We are not speaking here of 'going out together' as young lovers but of genuine friendship. Many groups are so lacking in their understanding of this that immediately a boy and a girl start even talking together the pressure is on for them to 'pair off'. As a consequence, many get pushed into relationships they were never looking for—while others feel forced to keep their distance and so lose out on the opportunity for friendship.

To have a special friend of the opposite sex is to say that you enjoy their company and their interests but you are no more exclusive in that relationship than you would be with someone of the same sex. The same goes for the level of physical contact. This is a relationship of friends, not lovers, and hence the level of physical contact should be no more than would be expressed to brothers or sisters in Christ.

Special friends do things together and talk together, because they like each other and share common interests or outlooks on life. You may have several specific friends of the other sex, some of whom may become friends of your future spouse as well and so last a lifetime. The important point is that you are agreed these relationships are no more than that.

Band three—going out together

One of these friendships may develop into love. Hopefully, by the time it does you are old enough for a serious relationship and could at least contemplate the possibility of marriage. It's not necessary or a good idea to go out with someone like this in your early teens.

If you sense the relationship changing, and one of the signs is that you both do, then you need to make a definite decision to 'move bands'. Falling in love is a very wonderful and spontaneous thing, but it doesn't take away our ability to think about what we're doing. By consciously deciding now 'to go out together' you keep your relationship secure.

What has happened is that you now want to be together, not just because you are friends, but precisely because you are of the opposite sex. This is the beginning of sexual love.

This level of relationship is obviously more intimate—and more physical. But we still need to recognise where it's at. The level of physical contact should be no more than that which is affectionate and therefore suitable for expressing in public. Anything which is overtly arousing is out! God gave sexual arousal as a prelude to intercourse, not as a way of saying goodnight.

This is time for long walks and much talking, for romantic meals, for sharing the discovery of young love. It isn't a licence for heavy petting. In fact, that will actually hinder the development of your love for each other and build in problems for later.

Band four—engagement

If you have entered responsibly into the previous level of relationship, it is highly likely that you will want to marry. There comes a time when you realise you cannot live without your girlfriend or boyfriend. You have fallen deeply and permanently in love. You know each other really well. Circumstances are such that you can now contemplate marriage in the not too distant future. It's time to pop the question and become engaged.

Engagement is a promise to make a promise. It is a commitment to get married. To our mind engagements shouldn't last too long. This is the home straight, the time necessary to make all the wedding arrangements. A ring isn't just a reserved notice to keep others off. Long engagements in any case do significantly add to the sexual pressures.

Band five—into marriage

All being well, we marry somebody we have got to know in a wider context, someone who is now our best friend, a person we have fallen passionately in love with, who has already committed themselves to us, so that come the wedding day we make our vows with absolute joy and conviction. Then we live happily ever after. At least, we get a good start, a firm foundation, which will enable us to build a successful marriage. The rest is a long story and not for this book!

The most neglected band in all this is the second—special friendship. So often it's overlooked because we've copied the secular idea that the only relationship possible with the opposite sex is in fact a sexual one.

But if you go straight into a 'band three relationship', and especially if you allow your physical relationship to be sexually arousing, you make a commitment greater than either of you are ready for. When the light dawns and it breaks up, both parties get very hurt. More young people leave churches through broken relationships than for any other reason.

There are other consequences. Churches are close communities. If everyone in the YP 'does the rounds' and petting is heavy, to put it bluntly, it results in a lot of shop-soiled goods. Can God really be happy with a situation in which the bride and groom have been physically too intimate with half of the guests at the wedding? We think not.

There's also the occasional embarrassing pregnancy to think of. Christians don't as a rule take precautions, because they never intend to have intercourse. If they did, it would be a commitment to premeditated sin. Guess who's most likely to fall accidentally—the Christian or the worldly-wise non-Christian?

What we're trying to show by all this is that it's possible to delay sexual awakening and at the same time enjoy the company of the opposite sex. Our model also provides a good way of ensuring successful marriages.

Whether you like our particular analogy or not, we think it important that you give your children some kind of framework for relationships. In addition to what we've already written, we should advise our kids not to go out with non-Christian boyfriends or girlfriends, ie 'band three relationships'. The reason is simple: the Bible teaches that we are not to be unequally yoked with unbelievers (2 Corinthians 6:14). To go out seriously with an unbeliever is to set yourself on a pathway which will lead to a costly disobedience.

Sometimes the unbeliever gets converted, but more often than not it's the believer who loses his or her faith. It's best to advise our kids to look for a good, Spirit-filled Christian with whom they can share this most important aspect of their lives.

One of the things that has struck us in talking to some Christian teenagers is how ignorant they are about sexual arousal. Most agree that sex before marriage is out, but few seem to have any idea about how far they should go.

In our book *A Touch of Love* we used the illustration of a fast-flowing river leading to a waterfall in order to describe the process of sexual arousal and intercourse. Our advice is that those not intending to have intercourse shouldn't let themselves get caught in the current. There is a divinely-given point of no return!

This means teaching our children what is or isn't sexually arousing. It doesn't mean they can have no physical contact. We suggested in the book that there are plenty of calm bywaters along this river. These represent the expression of sexual affection, the sort of thing you can do in public without embarrassing anyone. Let's guide our children into knowing the difference.

True love

All this may sound rather organised and far removed from the soaring passions of the romantic novels. Can we expect our inexperienced children to act so responsibly when all their school friends are pairing off at the Saturday night disco? How can they know if they're in love? Is it something you can control, anyway? What did you do when you were their age?

One of our daughters had her first proposal of marriage when she was twelve years of age! We hadn't even got to the volume control, let alone the graphic equaliser by then! Sometimes you just have to handle matters gently but firmly. Young teenagers still get the feelings we used to call 'calf-love'. It's as irrational as ever it was—but we must insist that it's not true love. That may involve some painful confrontation, loud protestation and angry tearfulness. Stick with it, long-suffering parent! You were like that once.

When they get older, the question becomes more serious. If your children are believers then they will be praying for a life partner of God's choice. How do they know it's true love, the real thing, God's will for their lives?

Are they true friends? As a married couple, we are each other's best friend. We share common interests from different perspectives—*very* different perspectives! We disagree as friends do, we argue like friends, we make up like friends. That was how it was when we were courting. More than that, of course, but it's an important part of our relationship.

If your children do not have a tested friendship, then they don't have a good basis for marriage. That's one of the reasons why we should encourage them to get to know their partner very well, both in a social context and in a special friendship, before entering a serious courtship.

It's no use marrying someone you don't like. We had a

guy come to us once. He said, 'I'm getting married in a few weeks' time. I've got a real problem. I think the girl I'm marrying is really ugly!'

It seemed somewhat late in the day for him to make this disconcerting discovery. We did all we could to help him appreciate her good points. Believing that the real person shines through the eyes, John suggested the fellow concentrate upon that part of her anatomy. To no avail. He replied that she was cross-eyed!

If only they had been friends. You never consider your friend ugly, even if he's got a face like a plate of stew. He's your friend! What spiritual nonsense it is to say, 'Cor, you aren't half ugly, but God said I've got to love you!'

Is there true romance in your child's relationship? We believe in it. John likes me to buy him roses and chocolates! He loves the notion of me fording streams, battling against wild winds, scaling desperate cliffs and throwing grappling irons over stern battlements, just to bring him a box of Milk Tray!

Seriously, does this fellow treat your daughter with real affection? Is he obviously caring for her? 'As now, so then' is very true in marriage. What takes place in courtship carries on. The person you marry is the person you marry. And although we all hope to improve as our relationships deepen, we remain essentially the same kind of people we set out as. If he's not a gentleman now, he probably never will be.

Make sure that the girl respects your son. Is she really concerned about him? Does she encourage him? Is she the sort of girl who is prepared to follow his lead, or does she have him in tow? In spite of all the talk about women's changing roles these days, is she going to create a good home? That doesn't mean she has to be a *Cordon Bleu* cook, just that she has the right sort of outlook on the domestic scene.

The essence of Christian love is sacrifice. When Paul wrote his marvellous piece on marriage in Ephesians 5 he said in effect, 'Husband lay down your life for your wife, just as Jesus laid down his life for the church.' He also instructed wives to sacrifice—to submit—to their husbands as to the Lord.

That is the nature of God's love. It is sacrificial. Is there the potential for mutual sacrifice in this intended marriage? Is there a love that puts itself out? Is there a love that is prepared to serve the other person?

These are the kinds of questions which test whether this is the love of a lifetime. They require honest answers.

Having said all this, none of us can guarantee that our children will get it right first go. Following the pattern of relationships which we've suggested above will make it more than likely that they do, but you can't be one hundred per cent sure when it comes to love.

Your child may in all sincerity enter a relationship prayerfully and thoughtfully, only to find that it doesn't work out. What are we to do? Do you remember the lifeboat illustration we used early on in this book? We must come to the rescue.

As the old song says, 'Breaking up is so very hard to do.' There will be tears and heartache, but better now than when it's too late and they've committed themselves to marriage. That would be a disaster.

All parents have a measure of anxiety about their children's future, especially concerning marriage. As Christian parents we must pray that God will not only keep our children pure but that he will also lead them to a partner of his choice. Happily, there are a multitude of testimonies to demonstrate that he does hear the cries of his children in this matter.

We live in a world where Babylon, that Mother of Harlots, is spreading a foul poison throughout the sexual lives of this generation. We must help our kids to understand the society in which they live. Our lives must demonstrate a godly alternative. By faith we can provide an antidote for the poison and raise sexually healthy teenagers.

The devil hates it. We may wonder why the attack has been so sexually orientated. It is because the Devil loathes the idea of blessing being passed from one generation to another. Every time that happens his own day of reckoning looms nearer.

Christian marriages produce Christian families. The number of the elect increases. (Not only by this means, of course. Many others come to the Lord through primary evangelism.) The return of the Lord is hastened, and with it the final destruction of Satan.

Little wonder he seeks to warp sexuality, to wreck marriages and to destroy children. That's why we've got to be steadfast in our faith—understanding his methods and overcoming him by the word of God and by our prayers.

Yet more homework

If you have not yet had a genuinely honest, open talk with your children about the birds and the bees then you should do so.

Even if you have, try discussing our views with them. You, and they, may disagree over some points. That doesn't matter too much. The important thing is that you are talking.

Part Four

Faith, Fellowship and the Future

14

Passing on the Flame

It's sometimes said there's no such thing as a teenager in the Bible, and if we mean by that the jeans-clad, Madonna-mad, exam-swotting, globe-trotting, disco-bopping creatures that we have produced, then we agree. You won't find them in the Bible!

At the same time the Scriptures do recognise the time of life which we call the teenage years. So when we encounter the word 'youth' in the Bible, we can equally read it as 'teenager'. Thus, for example, Psalm 119:9 can be paraphrased, 'How can a teenager keep his way pure? By living according to your word.'

Or Psalm 144:12 might be rendered, 'Then our sons in their teenage years will be like well-nurtured plants, and our teenage daughters will be like pillars carved to adorn a palace.'

The psalmist's prayer touches one of the deepest desires of any Christian parent's heart. It is that our children should come into our faith and grow to love the Lord, and serve his church for the whole of their days. The one thing that threatens to break our hearts more than anything else is that our children upon reaching adulthood may reject the faith of their fathers and go the way of the world.

It's not automatic that our kids should love the Lord

with all their hearts. The fact that we produced them does not guarantee their salvation. Any theology which says otherwise is unreal to experience and fails to take account of what the Scriptures teach. On top of that, it's downright dangerous—we can hardly afford to be complacent about their eternal destinies.

Our children need to hear the gospel and to respond to the claims of Jesus Christ upon their own lives. It's vital that they experience genuine conversion. They may not have lived lives of great social evil but they are still sinners in need of salvation. No one attains heaven on the basis of a decent upbringing—not even the Pharisees could manage it!

Childhood professions of faith can be very real and lasting. It was the case with all three of our children. But the gospel doesn't end with conversion. Jesus calls us to be his disciples. That means learning to be like him and to do his will in our adult lives. As our children progress through their teens they will be confronted repeatedly with the challenge of what this means for them.

These demands of Christ mustn't be watered down. There isn't a special, modified gospel for teenagers, any more than you find a special gospel for women, or for men, or for one-legged monkeys! Jesus calls every one of us to radical discipleship, total life commitment to him. And let's not forget that the disciples who first heard him were largely young men and women.

It's tempting to play upon the idealism and emotional susceptibilities of young people and to produce an evangelical easy believe-ism. A happy-go-lucky, gutless Christianity can give leaders some flattering instant results, but it'll all be over by the time the 'converts' reach their twenties. True Christianity is a life-changing call to sacrifice, devotion and heroic deeds. Let's not con our kids into accepting a plastic replica which will melt as soon as the heat comes on.

Parental responsibility

The prime responsibility for all this lies with us parents. Excellent as many YP leaders, youth camps and conferences are, we mustn't leave the job to them.

Deuteronomy 6:4–9 says,

> Hear, O Israel: The Lord our God, the Lord is one. Love the Lord your God with all your heart and with all your soul and with all your strength. These commandments that I give you today are to be upon your hearts. Impress them on your children. Talk about them when you sit at home and when you walk along the road, when you lie down and when you get up. Tie them as symbols on your hands and bind them on your foreheads. Write them on the door-frames of your houses and on your gates.

Every Christian agrees that we should love the Lord our God with all our being. But we must also impress these things upon our children, not in religious gatherings, but in the context of everyday life. This is the true religion of the wayside. The things of God should arise naturally in our conversation as we chat at our meal tables, as we walk or drive, when we're on holiday or traipsing round the supermarket.

Proverbs 22:6 says, 'Train a child in the way he should go, and when he is old he will not turn from it.' It's a double-edged verse. If you train a child faithfully in the ways of God, then when he is old he will not turn from it. But, if you train a child badly in the ways of God then when he is old he will not turn from that, either!

If you say, 'Well, we think kids should make their own decisions. We're not going to force religion down their throats. They can find out for themselves when they're old enough, if they want to,' then you are training a child in the way he should go—and when he is old he will not turn from it.

Parents with this attitude are training their children to believe that the Christian faith isn't really that important. Cleaning your teeth is important, so is eating your greens and going to school. But worshipping God is something you can take or leave.

If you've been a believer for some time, you will hopefully know better than this and will have taught your children the gospel of the grace of God. They will have learned to pray on your knee. You will have guided them in how to read the Scriptures and given them an understanding of the major truths. By now, they may know how to worship in the Spirit, how to serve the Lord and how to witness. Probably at some point your child has made a profession of faith.

All of that is good, but it isn't enough. We keep coming across adults who have had Christian upbringings but who for one reason or another fell away during their teenage years.

In the last century there was written, and often sung, a hymn which seems excruciatingly sentimental to us today. It was called *Where is my wandering boy tonight?* But the hymn reflected the anguish of many a parent whose child had rebelled against the faith. We may not sing the hymn any more, but there are still many prodigal sons, and anxious parents still grieve over their spiritually-wayward children.

Of course, you may be a very recent believer yourself. Your children may have come into the faith with you. One of the greatest difficulties you perhaps face is the unfamiliarity of being spiritual together. It can seem strange and embarrassing to commence talking about the

Lord when your life to date has excluded him. It's especially so for English people because, for some strange reason, religion is still an embarrassing topic of conversation.

But overcome this natural shyness and you have all the freshness of new-found faith to experience together. Both you and your children can enjoy the exciting adventure of discovering all about the Lord. Although you do not have the advantages of long Christian experience, you may nevertheless gain some wonderful insights as to what it means to be a Christian family. In fact, you may progress faster than some who have grown complacent because of their many years in the church.

However, if your child is an older teenager and still not a believer, you will have to be more cautious. It's no use imposing a religious veneer on the life of a household if your seventeen-year-old son doesn't want it. He will only react with anger and make life miserable for everyone.

He feels something strange and alien has happened to you. What he needs to know is that you are still the same parents who love him and share the common ground you have always shared. That's the best way to reach him for the Lord. No pressure, no imposition. Just love, friendship and normality. Whether he comes to the Lord or not may well depend, not on your ability to preach to him, but upon your success at becoming a better friend to him.

It is often heard from certain platforms today that our children will do greater exploits than we. In one sense that may be true. For example, our own children, like many others, were not only saved at an earlier age than we were, but they were baptised in the Spirit, speaking in tongues, prophesying, witnessing, having visions, seeing miracles, long before ever we got into those things.

We praise God for all the good things experienced by recent generations of children, but it will take more than this if they are to bring about a significant change in the spiritual climate of our nation. The road of Christian discipleship is long and not without its pitfalls. Triumphal songs may help the march, but our children, like us, still have to walk with their feet, not their mouths!

We can help them. There are certain common factors at work in teenage Christian lives. If we understand what these are and know how to feed into them at appropriate points, our children have every chance of coming through with flying colours.

Training and testing

In his first letter, the apostle John draws a parallel between natural growth and spiritual growth. Children in the faith, he says, know that God is their Father. They also know that their sins are forgiven. Fathers in the faith know 'him who is from the beginning', that is, they have a mature personal relationship with Christ, the Eternal One.

The intention is that we should progress from childhood to maturity. In order to do so, we have to pass through adolescence.

Whether we attain maturity in the faith or not depends on what we make of this phase in our spiritual development. So the apostle explains what characterises a good spiritual teenager: 'I write to you, young men, because you are strong, and the word of God lives in you, and you have overcome the evil one' (1 John 2:14b).

The illustration applies whatever our natural age might be. It's to do with how much we have actually grown in the faith, not just the number of years we have been alive as Christians. We've met folk who have been forty years in the faith and yet have never come out of their nappies. Others, though converted only a short while, grow by leaps and bounds.

The reasons for this vary. Some remain immature

because the level of teaching in their churches never gets beyond the breast-milk stage—comforting, nutritious in its way, but not suited to spiritual adulthood. Others refuse the discipline of spiritual adolescence and so never develop the capacity for a mature relationship with Christ.

Although we say spiritual growth isn't simply to do with the number of years we've been around, nonetheless there is a certain parallel. For example, if your children gave their lives to the Lord at quite a young age, then it's entirely possible that the challenge of spiritual adolescence will hit them at the same time as they enter their natural teens.

Teenage years are spiritually a time of exercise, a season of battle training, and a period during which their minds are being renewed by the word of God. It's a time, if you like, when they are winning their spurs. This is when they must qualify to become true disciples of Jesus.

If all goes well, they will come through no longer fickle or naïve in their faith but with the steadfastness of those who have been properly coached for spiritual warfare.

Every teenage Christian has to engage the Enemy during this time. The conflict is usually on one specific topic. It will appear to be a major issue for the one enduring it.

Sometimes the testing is in the sexual realm—a fight with lustful masturbation, pornography, or heavy petting. It can be over a boyfriend or a girlfriend. Or it may come as a lure to covet something. An obsessive craving for a motorbike or an expensive stereo, for example. Your child may even be tempted to steal.

The battle may be in the realm of personal identity—pride or on the other hand self-pity and inadequacy. Some children wrestling with these issues are tempted into taking drugs—cigarettes, alcohol abuse, glue-sniffing, cocaine, 'pot' or heroin. If you suspect this then you need to act fast if a tragedy is to be averted.

Whatever the trial, the outcome is crucial to our children's spiritual future. Yet, for all our care and concern, we may hardly be aware that the battle is taking place.

Jesus went into the wilderness for his fight with the Enemy. Nobody saw, nobody helped or comforted. It was his battle. On three key issues—the lust of the flesh, the lust of the eyes and the pride of life—the devil tested him. There could be no 'destroying the works of the Evil One' in the lives of others until the Son of God had proved that those works could not take control of his own life.

He overcame by the word of God, and sent the Devil scuttling. It wasn't the end of the war, but the battle was a crucial one. Jesus returned from it in the power of the Spirit, ready now to wreak havoc on Satan's kingdom and to usher in a new era of salvation.

So it must be with our children. They have to learn in their own experience that they can win. It's a bit like taking on the playground bully. Sooner or later, this young thug gets to duff up everyone in the class. Your Johnny is wondering when his turn is going to come. Then one day the bully shoves into him. 'Oi! Who're you pushing? Looking for a fight, are you? Right, I'm going to punch your face in!'

There's no one else to hand. Your little kid has to handle this alone. If he runs, he's only putting off the evil day. If he quails, the bully will win and continue to terrorise him for life. What's he to do?

He may be frightened stiff on the inside, but outwardly he sets his jaw. 'All right, then. If that's what you want.' And before the bully can make a further move, *wham,* your kid gives him a right-hook in the midriff. Down goes the thug! (It will help if your child has prepared somewhat for this eventuality!)

That bully will respect your child in the future; he knows he packs a punch. More importantly, little Johnny no longer lives in fear and trepidation; he knows that this bully isn't as tough as he makes out.

In spiritual terms, children have to learn the power of the word of God and the sword of the Spirit over against the subtle reasonings and violent threatenings of the Devil.

When John writes, 'And the word of God lives in you,' he means that the word which is written on the page of a Bible has become prophetic; it has become the living word of the Spirit in our own hearts. God's word is now ours also.

Let's illustrate it this way. A man used to shoplift before he was saved. He did not stop shoplifting simply because the Bible says, 'Thou shalt not steal.' New Covenant faith isn't a matter of looking up the rules and thinking, 'I mustn't do that any more,' and then engaging in a lifelong fight with our own desires. The new birth works something much more powerful in us: 'I will write my laws on their hearts.'

When a regenerate man reads the truth, the Holy Spirit witnesses it to his renewed spirit. The man agrees in his heart that shoplifting is wrong. He himself no longer wants to do it. He has come to agree with God. God's word has become his word. Not mere outward conformity but inner conviction.

During this time our children will learn what this means for themselves. Truth we have taught them will begin to make sense in their experience. The choice as to which voice they obey will bring into focus the true desires of their hearts.

As with all times of training, there are good days and bad days. Remember when you were trying to pass exams? One day you'd sit down and it actually seemed interesting. You'd study and things made sense. Some of it even went in. Another day you'd stare at the book and think, 'I've been reading that line for an hour now, and I still don't know what it says, let alone what it means!'

The same is true when you're training for a sport. There are days when everything goes right and those when everything goes wrong. One day you wish this were the championship because you're performing so well. The next, you feel you'd be better off taking up crochet instead.

It's just the same spiritually. Our children will have their ups and their downs. Sometimes they will make enormous strides in a very short time. At others, they will seem hardly to have started at all. That's typical of any training time in life.

Part of learning is, of course, finding out for oneself. The insecure person is frightened to experiment for fear of getting it wrong. But those who make no mistakes seldom make anything at all. Experimenting and taking risks is what progress is all about.

When we bought our computer, we went through the manual very, very carefully, step by step, frightened that we were going to wipe the programme out at any minute. When our Steve gets on the computer, he doesn't even bother with the manual. In half an hour he's mastered most of it, anyway. Bang, bang, bang on the keyboard, 'Try this, Dad. No, try that. It doesn't matter if you lose it 'cos you can still get it out of limbo. What we need is an integer-expression to poke in a goto loop so that we can chain merge with the option base. Otherwise we'll never get the array subscript to run.' If this sounds like gibberish....

Steve learned by experiment. He was less fearful of getting it wrong than we were, so he knows more—about computers, anyway!

In the spiritual realm this can give us anxious parents some worries. For example, your child may suddenly decide not to go to church one Sunday. He wants to go out with some mates instead. Holy panic! Is this the end of his faith? Or is it just an experiment? You may even find out that he sacrificed going to church in order to try and win his friends to the Lord. A right fool you'll feel if you start an earnest exhortation about 'not forsaking the gathering together of yourselves' the moment he walks in the door, only to find out that his friends are coming with him to church the following Sunday!

She might want to go to another church. A church not like yours, heaven forbid! What's going on? Just another experiment. As likely as not your daughter will return full of enthusiasm: 'Isn't our church wonderful! I never knew it was so good until I tried that other place. It was so boring! I'm not going there again.'

Of course, she might have found it much better! In which case, you've got something to learn about the reasons why.

However painful it is for us, when they appear not to be reading their Bibles, not praying, not wanting to go to church, not enjoying the worship, sitting in the back row chewing gum, we've got to let it happen. They must find out for themselves what they want. Certainly, it's inappropriate by the time a child reaches fifteen or sixteen years of age still to be dictating their leisure time on these matters.

What they are asking themselves is, 'Do I really need this faith? Do I really want this lifestyle?' Quite likely the Devil is asking them those questions, too—and offering some juicy alternatives. Pray for them.

Where are the role models?

We've already mentioned that we think teenagers need a good sexual role model in Mum and Dad. But they are looking for role models in all aspects of life. Hence the success of the cults. One of the major reasons why teenagers become enmeshed in cults such as the Moonies is because there exists a charismatic personality at the top.

What kind of role model are you? Teenage years, more than any other time, will test and expose hypocrisy in the home. As we've indicated throughout this book, they are watching our behaviour like hawks. They are challenging to see whether our faith is good enough; whether it's true, or whether it's false.

And they will tell us off! It's an uncomfortable experience, and one which we will be tempted to resent. When children are young, if they tell you off or accuse you of anything, you rebuke them. 'Don't be rude! Don't you dare speak like that to your mum. If you do it again you'll get a good hiding!' But when they become teenagers you've got to listen—not to blatant and unwarranted rudeness, but to what they're picking up. 'You're always so rotten miserable at teatime, Dad. All you do is moan. It's the same every day.'

Tempted as you are to retort, 'Don't you speak to me like that! How dare you say I'm miserable!' you must hold your tongue because they are probably right. Six o'clock in the evening is a bad time for many of us. Worn out from work, being depressed by the news, trying to eat your meal, and they want to ask questions about whether they can go with some friends to Finland in October, whether you will pay for it, and whether you will arrange for someone to drive them to the airport at three o'clock in the morning because it's a cheap flight and won't cost you so much money if you do that.

It's no easy matter to move from demanding a proper respect from your children to having to repent because they've actually spotted something inconsistent in your Christian life. It's much easier to go back to the old defensive role model of parent and young child than to say, 'Sorry! I guess you're right.'

Teenagers observe, and they say what they feel. A good deal of the time they will be devastatingly right. It's uncomfortable, but you've got to take it. Take note: if you are carnal, then why should they be spiritual? If you cannibalise the preacher over Sunday lunch, then why should they ever respond to the word of God? If you criticise people in the church who are not doing it right in your eyes, is it surprising that your kids grow cynical about those same people, and develop fault-finding attitudes?

They are looking for consistency and reality in their parents, so it's no use going all religious and plastering every wall and shelf with texts. Nor is it any help to adopt a pious super-spirituality. 'Hallelujah, the milk's boiled over!' 'Praise the Lord, Johnny's just fallen down stairs and broken his leg!' Choruses all day long will drive your kids barmy. 'Hallelujah anyway,' or the more refined, 'The Lord knows,' when the tank bursts, the door falls off its hinges, you trip over the cat and bring the washing down on your head, will turn them off. Especially if on other matters you are less 'spiritual'.

What's really needed is a consistent demonstration of spiritual integrity and honesty in the home. That means being open about our faults as well as our good points.

Children are impressed, not by our chorus singing, our platitudes and texts, but by our humility and our willingness to say, 'I've got that wrong. I'm sorry.' They are blessed when we make the long journey up to their room, where they are sitting reading a book with some head-banging music pounding through their brains, lift off the ear-phones and say, 'Sorry I was ratty down there. I didn't mean to be, but I was. Please forgive me!'

Our ability to be honest over our failures is more

important, we believe, than any other single factor. Kids really can't cope with hypocrisy and double standards in their parents. Honesty truly is the best policy at home—and everywhere else!

This isn't to say that our children always get it right, or that we should for ever be telling them how bad we are. Part of the problem of youth is simply the lack of experience and perspective on life. But they get more right than our parental pride likes to admit, and we will do well to try and learn from their observations, even if they are a little over the top at times. In fact, your teenagers can be a greater means of bringing conviction to you about where you need to improve than all the sermons your pastor preaches in a year!

All this is more important than our texts and choruses—and even family Bible studies. As families grow up it becomes quite difficult, if not impossible, to maintain a 'family altar'. In the past, you may have liked to gather for a reading and prayer at the breakfast table. Now everyone gets up and leaves the house at different times. If your child doesn't have to go to school that day, he may not get up at all!

One of the practical things we try to do every so often (it has to be said with limited success), is to break bread together as a family. Sometimes it can be done by making Sunday lunch the one good family meal when we're together.

If family prayers are no longer practicable, then praying for one another at all sorts of other times is vital. We pray for each other whenever there's something that needs praying about. We don't wait for a family time or a special moment in the day. On the stairs, in our rooms, by the kitchen sink, we pray for and with one another. The Lord is real and he's not confined to meetings over the meal table or meetings in church.

The best role models our children can have is of parents who are honest, genuine believers who quite naturally bring the Lord into all aspects of their daily life, without recourse to any form of religious artificiality. Children of such parents will always feel they can talk about their own spiritual experiences without embarrassment or fear. They will learn how to be naturally supernatural.

Others will have their part to play, of course. Youth leaders, pastors, respected Christians will all have something to contribute. And it's good for our children to be exposed to the influence of truly godly people. But there's no substitute for our role as parents.

15

Spiritual Awareness

Oh, the joy of young glands and open minds! Excitable, energetic teenagers awash with hormones at the merest stimulus of the Spirit. Ready to go to the ends of the earth, to change the world, to topple the giants and usher in the kingdom of God. Not for nothing did Peter proclaim, 'Your sons and daughters will prophesy, your young men will see visions' (Acts 2:17). No spiritual sexism here! Upon your teenagers, girls and boys, will I pour my Spirit, says the Lord.

While old men dream, youngsters are getting hyped-up with visions of a glorious future. Their zeal may well make us feel our age.

You have only to watch them in their meetings. Young Christians praise God very, very energetically these days. They're jumping up and down, shouting, 'Praise the Lord, yeah, yeah, glory to God!' You're bracing your legs for one feeble hop, gasping, 'Puff, pant, yeah, puff, glory!' as best you can.

We were in a meeting recently where at the appeal hundreds of young people surged forward. It was not a young people's meeting as such and when a member of the platform party asked, 'Hey, what about the old ones?' there were hundreds of older folk who put their hands up as those who should also have come forward. The teenagers demonstrated more zeal for God, more honesty, less self-consciousness about whether they would be 'looked at' than did the older people. That is typical of teenage years. It's possible to obtain incredible responses from them because they are so open and enthusiastic.

But they're still immature. And, as we've stressed already, it's no sin to be so. The difficulty for us parents is that there will often appear to be a contradiction between the vision that our children are getting at church and the fact that they won't tidy their rooms.

'Cor, Mum, we had a fantastic time at YP tonight. It was incredible! We laid hands upon everybody; we all felt hot and cold and shivery inside and Bill freaked out on the floor for half an hour, Mum. We stood around him holding our hands over him, he was laughing and chuckling and he was flinging his arms, and then Sheila—she screamed like mad and started dancing round the room. It was fantastic!'

'Done your homework?'

'Aw, Mum! I haven't had time. You know that. And I don't have to do it until next Thursday.'

'I thought you said it had to be in tomorrow?'

'Wellll. Well, he's a lousy teacher, anyway.'

'But you need to study for exams and a job.'

'Aw, come on, Mum. You never get a job when you leave school, anyway. What's the point of bothering with it? Besides, I'm going to be a missionary after tonight, and I don't need to work for that! You're always going on at us about our homework. I'm fed up with it and I'm going to bed. So there!'

What happened to the glorious time at YP?

How we handle this all-too-familiar scene is ever so crucial. It's tempting to come down on them and to wipe out that spiritual experience as being totally over the top and unrealistic. Sheer hypocrisy and all that. But do we really want to knock their admittedly immature expressions of faith? Should we not be grateful that they're showing their enthusiasm for God rather than for the local football club or some vain pop star?

Earlier in the book we said we would explain why Christian young people find the lure of romanticism and rock so hard to resist. The reason is simple. Rock culture offers emotional satisfaction. Its images, the driving beat, the chance to dance, the hype and glamour—it's exciting. A rock concert is a corporate 'spiritual' experience, a celebration of life and energy, an occasion of cosmic worship. Compare that to your average church service!

Unless our children can be allowed to experience emotionally the reality of God in their lives, we'll lose them to the prevailing alternative—or they'll grow up deadly dull. Whatever we might make of modern trends in Christian worship, there's no doubt that freer styles have greatly helped our young people to feel they have something going for them that's every bit as good as the rock culture. In fact, most of them will say it's far better.

But it still won't guarantee tidy rooms or completed homework.

This ability to have incredible feelings and experiences, yet somehow not to connect these with the reality of homework and room tidying, is simply a matter of immaturity. It's actually only a teenage version of what is true in so many of our lives.

We can go to church and praise the Lord with all our hearts, but what happens when we get back for lunch? The meat is underdone—or incinerated. Husband stomps up the garden muttering something about starvation. Wife resents the fact that he didn't even lay the table. 'Cutlery will be rusty by the time we get to eat at this rate,' he mutters. She reaches for the tin of baked beans. 'Serves you right!' she fumes. What's so different? Except that we should know better, and the word 'sin' probably should be applied to our reactions.

It's the same as going to work on Monday morning and finding the whole office or factory is in chaos and people haven't done what they should have done. You're feeling fed up, cheesed off with the whole thing and it shows. That's only the adult version of immaturity. We all have to learn how to connect our spiritual experience with the reality of our daily lives. The last thing you want from your husband or boss is, 'Call yourself a Christian? You rotten hypocrite!'

Our kids can do without it as well. Here's a better approach: 'Darling, it's terrific that you had such a good time at YP tonight. I'm glad you enjoyed it so much. Let's pray that God will enable you to take that into school tomorrow and demonstrate it in your work and in your relationships.'

'Oh, er, oh, all right, Mum. Yeah! Well, I was just going to go to bed now. I'm feeling quite tired.'

'Well, we'll just pray about that. Let's ask God that the things the Spirit is doing will enable you to do your homework. Let's pray that somehow the Holy Spirit will have an effect upon your room. After all, you don't want the angels tripping over everything, do you?'

You'll probably get a wry smile do acknowledge that they've got the hint.

Speaking of rooms, how many parents have arguments with their kids about the state of their bedrooms? Probably more cross words are exchanged over this than almost any other subject. Many of those words are needless.

It may help to know that there are, broadly speaking, two types of mind in this world. We'll call them the mind of the accountant and the mind of the artist. Those with the former tend to think in tidy compartments, in neatly stored boxes, in order. They make excellent researchers, being superb at fine detail, accuracy and the like. You want a surgeon who thinks like that! Such people probably have tidier rooms than most of us.

Those with the artist's mind think associatively. Their heads are a dustbin full of ideas and memories all thrown in together. But just say the right word and it will connect up with the thing you want. These are the creative thinkers, the people of ideas and insight. They make good prophets. They are seldom tidy.

Most of us are a mixture of both types of mind and, without overstating it, are usually mid-range when it comes to tidiness.

Here's the point. What is more important, that things are laid out neatly and in order, or that we can find what we want when we need to? And that's the test of whether your child's room is actually chaos or is in fact an associative but workable jumble. Can they come up with the goods? Does the homework turn up? Or is it always lost first thing Monday morning? Can they come out dressed reasonably clean. Are you sure there are no mice and strange coloured things growing down the walls, or under the bed?

We're not suggesting you give your children licence to live in chaos, and certainly not in filth, but we do recommend you allow them to express their own mind in the way that they live. All of us appreciate a bit of space that we can call our own and in which we can be ourselves.

We suggest that you might make a reasonable house rule that at least an hour a week is spent on cleaning and tidying the room, including returning other people's things that they have borrowed. That will keep the mess down and the morale up. And when you conduct room inspection try not to say, 'What a tip! Have you done *anything* in the last hour?' Unless it's true, of course. And the way to check that out is to inspect before and after.

This time of spiritual awareness mustn't be despised. God will work many things in their lives during these years and although we may wince at times, we should not be too judgemental. Better your children get high on Jesus than on drugs or sex or violence.

And there will be a genuineness about their faith which can be quite startling.

The other day our daughter, Sharon, and her fiancé arrived home at our nearest railway station, three miles away, only to find they had no money to phone for a cab, let alone to pay the taxi fare. So they prayed.

The woman in front of them at the phone booth said there was 15p credit left if they wanted it. That took care of the phone call! The taxi duly arrived and just as they were getting in, penniless, a stranger approached, enquired as to their destination, found it was on his route, asked if he could share their cab, and said he would pay the fare in full! Not bad, eh?

Questions, questions, questions

Some churches seem to be nothing but questions. Questions about doctrine, questions about the way the pastor runs the show, questions about unanswerable speculations, questions about what the YP get up to. The one thing not permitted is a clear, authoritative answer.

Other churches, particularly those which have embraced a certain form of authority/submission teaching, may not permit questions at all. Doctrine is as delivered, the church is run as the elders dictate, all initiatives come from the top. Even though such churches do not as a rule impose their authority in a cultish manner, nonetheless, creative investigation is at a low premium among the membership.

Ideally, a church should recognise both the place of spiritual authority and the place of exploratory learning.

People should not be in rebellion but nor should they be discouraged from asking intelligent questions.

We need to engender such attitudes in our teenagers. Certainly, we must beware of panicking or becoming overly defensive when they want to ask serious questions about the faith.

Teenagers' spiritual questions tend to fall into three broad categories: those about what the Bible actually means, those concerning the big social issues of the day, and those to do with the life of the church.

The first sort are fairly easy to deal with. If you don't know the answer yourself, refer them to a good Bible dictionary or commentary. Failing that, recommend them to speak with the pastor. After all, he's meant to be the expert!

The second kind are more difficult. For example, a common question they might ask is: 'If there's a God of love, if he really loves, then why does he allow all this suffering in the world?' Or the other version of the same problem: 'If God is all-powerful, more powerful than the Devil, why doesn't he stop the evil that's going on?'

Fair questions. And it's proper that they should be asked. Our children are trying to relate their faith at its interface with everyday world experience. They're not simply rebelling and we mustn't treat them as though they were. Instead, we must seek to answer them with the simplicity of wisdom.

For example, when there's a disaster such as the Townsend Thoresen ferry tragedy, you could respond by saying, 'Isn't the Devil evil to do that, but isn't God good that it happened on a sand-bank and not more were lost? And didn't he inspire so many courageous people who managed to get there and do such wonderful work in saving people's lives? Oh, and isn't man arrogant that he gets so careless about his own abilities that he doesn't put sufficient safety checks into his operations?'

That's relating faith and experience. It's not answering the whole question of why God allowed the thing to happen in the first place. We don't pretend to have an easy answer to that one! But it is a way of broadening out the initial question so that our children can see there's more to it than meets the eye. It won't do simply to blame God!

Take the Ethiopian famine as another example. You might approach it like this: 'Aren't we arrogant in this country? We have more than enough food. In fact, there is enough food to feed every mouth in the world but we are so greedy and selfish as a society that we let these people starve. We could easily afford to ship out millions of tons of grain to them, but we won't do it. Instead, we're cutting back on our farming, we're reducing our output because we're too efficient and producing too much. Rather than give it to the poor, we're reducing the amount that we produce. Isn't that evil?'

Help your children to see where the real problem is. The West has failed to see that its ability to produce an excess of food is a stewardship from God to enable the starving to be fed as well. That's sin!

And the answer to sin lies not in violent political revolution but in the transforming power of the gospel. Not only do individuals need it but so does society as a whole. We must challenge this wretched institutional evil with the love and mercy of God. Get out there and start sharing it, kids!

Answers of this kind provide our children with a bit more ammunition for the debates they encounter at school and college. And they are reassured themselves that their faith is relevant to the modern world.

The range of social questions is vast and undoubtedly confronts the church with its major challenge for the next decade. Let's not be afraid to give our children militant answers. After all, this is spiritual warfare.

The third kind of question revolves around church life. Why are things run the way they are? What's wrong with Mrs Jones? Why doesn't our church allow this, that or the other? These are the most sensitive questions, for they draw us in at the level of our own prejudices and opinions. Wise restraint is called for, as well as honesty. It's all too easy to allow our own feelings to colour the answer we give, especially if we ourselves are dissatisfied with the way things are going. A bit of intelligent criticism on our part may be interpreted by them as permission to dynamite the pulpit!

For all that, don't discourage their questions and observations. They can often see things with clearer eyes than we can. One of our children once devasted us with an observation about the worship in our previous church. He said, 'Dad, where's the Holy Spirit gone in our church? Our worship is just a chorus sandwich.'

We were taken aback. We'd not used such a phrase in our child's living memory. In fact, we had last used it in about 1972 when we had abandoned hymn-sandwich type services in favour of a freer and more biblical pattern.

But our son had perceived that things had slipped into another rut. It drove us to prayer. Steve wasn't rebelling, he was perceiving. We needed to seek the Lord over it and pray, 'Lord, let your Spirit move again. Let us not settle for a new liturgy. Let us not come into another kind of routine that neglects the Holy Spirit.'

Let the questions come. Both parents and children can learn from them. And if we feel ill-qualified to give the right answer, let's ask God for wisdom. Unlike intellectual expertise which depends upon intelligence, wisdom is given to all who ask—and often the less intelligent, not relying on their own understanding, receive a whole lot more than the brainy ones. A comforting thought for all of us!

16

The Will of God

Do your children know the purpose of God for their generation? Are you able to tell them what it is, or even to enable them to discover it for themselves?

Although there may be some differences of opinion over what has constituted the will of God for our own generation, some things are reasonably clear. (We take it that God is not helplessly looking on while we mess around with our own petty ideas. He is the Lord of history, and of his church in particular.) For example, there has been a considerable rediscovery of worship by the Spirit in the past twenty years. Although the forms have varied from church to church, there is no major grouping of churches left untouched.

A renewed emphasis upon the work of the Spirit in the life of the believer, and the re-emergence of spiritual gifts should also be noted. It has led a significant number of churches to adopt new and arguably more biblical structures of life together, not least including the release of the laity to minister in areas such as home groups. And a fresh challenge to re-evangelise the nation is coming rapidly to the fore. There is much else besides.

If you have been an active Christian for any length of time you will have been, to some degree or other, a part of all this. But, good as it may have been for us, it does not constitute the will of God for our children. We must beware of simply putting them through an action replay of our own history. That would be to turn their Christian lives into a game of charades.

In the progressive church tradition from which we come, our children do not have to discover how to replace legalistic quiet times with Spirit-filled devotions. It's not necessary for them to find out how to substitute vibrant worship for the hymn sandwich. They don't need to be taught about house groups and Ephesians 4:11 ministry patterns. All these matters were the concern of our earlier years.

Time rolls on, the issues change, the lines of battle move. This up-and-coming generation needs to hear God for itself. Proverbs 29:18 says, in the Authorised Version, 'Where there is no vision, the people perish.' And it's true. If we wonder why teenagers sometimes seem bored with church, it's because they have no vision. Nobody has effectively communicated with them what their part is in the purposes of God.

When we were young believers, once we knew our spiritual role we were gripped. Nothing else mattered. All our energies went into fulfilling this glorious challenge. So it must be for our children. They need to know the hand of the Lord upon them for their own generation. Otherwise, the present widespread awakening will fail and yet another spiritual revolution will be needed to mobilise the church for the hour.

The problem is even more acute for those in traditional churches. Thousands of young people grow up in Sunday schools, attend youth organisations and church services, but never make it to adult church membership. Why? Because nothing gripped them.

We do not have the space to enlarge upon what we think

God's purpose is for this new generation of Christians, nor is it altogether appropriate that we should, because teenagers must feel themselves to be part of the process of discovery. They don't simply want to be told what their elders think they should do.

However, it most certainly requires them to get very much more involved in society than we have. They will have to take on the powerful institutions in our land. In the process, they will almost certainly experience levels of persecution different from those we have encountered. A resurgence of mission is called for, but of a totally new style, both in this land and throughout the world.

We can encourage our children to explore these matters with one another. Teach them that the Christian life isn't just a hobby. Most important of all, assure them that they have a role to play in the future of the church, and it starts now.

This broad perspective perhaps concerns church leaders more than parents, though we have our part to play. But what about the specific will of God for our children's individual lives? What about studies and careers?

Success and sacrifice

Do we expect our children to succeed? What do we mean by success? How is it measured? Many Christian parents come from rather middle-class backgrounds or have evolved into middle-class lifestyles as a result of conversion.

It's trendy to knock this, and usually the people doing so are themselves middle class. Not having the courage to forsake their comfortable lifestyle themselves, perhaps they shout righteously about the virtues of working-class Christianity to appease their consciences!

But consider this for a moment. You may have been a

debtor with no idea of how to manage money, no wisdom to speak of, and then you became a Christian. You committed your financial state to God and he gave you wisdom. You began to give to his work and he started honouring you. Before you knew it, you were out of debt and saving. Gradually, your lifestyle began to improve, quite naturally. You've become comfortably well off. Because you appreciate that it's by the grace of God, you probably handle this with a good spirit.

There's nothing wrong with it. In fact, it's a testimony! However, the problem may come with your children. They have inherited your comfortable standard of living, quite likely with no real appreciation that it came about as a direct result of living by faith. The danger is that they will simply adopt secular middle-class values and expectations as the way things are.

Do we give them to expect that success means automatically buying a house rather than renting or living on a council estate? Is it understood that they are going to get nine GCSEs and three 'A' levels, go to university or college, have a good middle-class job? Is that what we mean by success? Or are we open to the possibility that the will of God might be rather different?

We are not adopting some pseudo-left-wing position by saying this. Nor are we anti-success. We believe God calls people to be very successful and go to the top. Indeed, we pray that Christians reach positions of real power and influence in our society. And every good parent, quite rightly, hopes their children will do well in life.

But we must be careful that we don't just lay our values unthinkingly on our children. Supposing the Lord calls them to lay down their lives for the gospel? At a recent conference John brought a prophetic word concerning forsaking everything that you have in order to follow Jesus. He did his best to make the appeal as difficult as possible to respond to. He tried to get folk to sit down even after they had stood. He emphasised the cost.

For all his efforts, a large number of young people responded very seriously to the call. But the real cost for many was to do with their Christian parents.

John had young people coming to him in tears the next day saying, 'I wanted to stand, but I couldn't pay the price of how my Christian mum and dad would respond to the idea of me giving up everything for God. They have career expectations for me and would be appalled at the idea of me being a single missionary, possibly even losing my life for Jesus. I'm not afraid to do those things for him, but I know how my parents will feel.'

It demonstrated the spiritual depth of some of those young people that they feared they might have missed the boat by not standing up the previous night. One guy said, 'I would want to stand up now 'cos I've prayed this through overnight. I've agonised with God and I'm prepared even to take on the antagonism of my parents. Can I be counted in among those who stood to lay down their lives for the Lord?' Yes, he could. And difficult as his parents might find it, they had actually done a fine job in producing such character in their son.

We mention this, not to frighten every parent who reads these pages, but because we recognise the seriousness of the call of God upon some young people's lives. A number may even die for the Lord. Some of them will give up that career and those qualifications. It will mean sacrificing marriage for some—and that means no grandchildren, Mum!

This is not necessarily going to be the will of God for everybody by a long chalk. For many people, his purpose is that they get married, live in the same sort of house as you, and have kids just like you. That's as much a part of the kingdom of God. What we're calling for is a willingness on our part to release our children into whatever God has for them—and that may not be 'success' as the world counts it.

We must remind ourselves that years ago we dedicated our children to the Lord. We said, 'Lord, thank you for the gift of this child. We return the gift to you, and we receive from you a stewardship to raise him for you.' Whatever the words, that's what we meant. Our children's possible futures may now test the truth of our promises.

Career choices

Once our own hearts are clear on this, we are in a position to guide, help and advise our teenagers. We must talk through study options, career possibilities and work opportunities. By all means, let's take advantage of the Careers Office and any other advice to hand, but we need to be involved, too. After all, we know our children very well! And, most importantly, we can bring in the vital spiritual dimension concerning the will of God.

We need to discuss matters with our children's teachers, as well. Parents' evenings are useful, but don't be afraid to call in at other times. A good teacher appreciates your interest; a bad one needs it. Mind you, your child may well complain like mad about you interfering and do his best to put you off going.

'It's no use seeing Mr Cobblebrain. He's thick! He doesn't even know who I am. Anyway, whatever he says, it's because he's mixed me up with someone else. And you won't understand what he's talking about, anyway. Come to think of it, he left last term, and the new teacher's deaf and dumb, so I don't even know his name!'

Take not a blind bit of notice. Mr Cobblebrain will probably turn out to be charming, passably intelligent, and even quite helpful!

The number of choices today is quite bewildering. And the pressure to specialise early on is a very real one. For this reason we shouldn't be worried if our children can't make up their minds what they're going to do in life. Indeed, the chopping and changing of ideas is quite a healthy process. Far better that than to be like the girl who has made up her mind from childhood that she's going to be a nurse, only to find that she isn't accepted at the interview, and then is left completely without a clue as to her future.

In spite of the apparent pressure to get everything sewn up, it's perfectly possible for teenagers to change courses, take a short-lived job or two, and still get it right in the end. We must be careful not to stream our children too narrowly, too early.

One of the acid tests of any study course or career choice must be, 'Do you really enjoy the work?' That's not to say it won't be hard at times, but is it generally enjoyable? There's little point in a child struggling with a subject if he really doesn't like it in the first place.

We've found these questions useful to ask our children when we've had periodic talks about their futures. You may think of others.

1. What do you like doing?
2. What are you good at doing?
3. Do you prefer to work alone or in a team?
4. Do you want to produce a product or work with people?
5. What sort of working environment do you favour?
6. Do you want a manual or a desk job?
7. What do you think God is saying?

Such questions help bring clarity. It's then a matter of exploring the possibilities together. And as you do so, encourage your children to pray continually, 'Your will be done.'

Actually finding a job is a story in itself. The possibility frankly depends a lot on which part of the country you live in. Unemployment is a real threat to many and the constant struggle to find work can totally destroy a teenager's self-confidence.

Children need our support and prayers at such times. They also need our encouragement not to mope around all day but to find useful things to do. Churches in depressed areas really ought to construct voluntary work programmes, and even small businesses, for their unemployed young people.

Many children have no problem at all and quite enjoy the challenge of applications and interviews. Most still appreciate a few tips on how to go about it. Today, presentation and self-confidence are quite as important as qualifications. That's where we parents come in.

Before full-time work commences you may have to face the vexed issue of their getting a part-time job while still at school. The money, of course, will be welcomed by all—you especially as it means you can stop shelling out a small fortune in pocket money. But it does need to be weighed against other things, such as how your child is doing at school, how tired he gets, the impact a job is going to make on his social life, and so forth.

You may have to resist the pressure for a while until the right sort of job comes up. And even when and if you give in, keep an eye on things. Many bosses exploit juveniles in ways that are actually illegal and it can bring your children under real pressure.

Discouragement

You may be reading this and saying to yourself, 'It must be great to have children who are spiritually aware, asking questions, finding out the will of God for their lives. But my kids aren't like that at all. They're bored silly with the whole business! What am I to do?'

Just about all kids go through phases of unresponsiveness. Usually, it's because they have grown discouraged with life. There are several reasons why this might be.

Overdemand

It's surprising how many teenagers there are, from both Christian and non-Christian homes, who feel they've fallen short of expectations.

Christian young people may feel they should be more spiritual. Although their parents have never vocalised it, they pick up a sense that they've let the side down. If studies have been linked with spirituality then they may feel a disappointment in their schoolwork as well. Often this feeling of failure is particularly with regard to the father.

It's so important that we reassure our children that they're all right. For example, we have always made it clear to our kids, when they're taking exams, that if they succeed we'll say, 'Praise the Lord!' And if they fail, we'll still say, 'Praise the Lord!'

We have never given them grounds to imagine that their acceptance depended upon their passing exams. Yet even so, such is the pressure today, that they have on occasions felt it was so. We all have to work hard at constantly reassuring our children of our unconditional love for them.

The same goes for spiritual or physical performance. Worship and service must spring from the heart, not from a desire to gain acceptance with parents. Sporting or musical accomplishment is very fine, but we must beware of using their standing with us as a lever to make them perform better. 'We'll be so proud of you if you win,' carries with it the unspoken consequence, 'We'll be so disappointed in you if you lose.' It's a wrong pressure to lay on our children.

Let your kids know that you accept them because you love them—and that's good enough! Keep telling them that, because they live in an age and at a time of life when people are making great demands and are often putting them down.

We've been appalled, for example, by teachers who have made children feel worthless because they didn't come up to their expectations of them. That is so evil. Teachers who use cynicism and sarcasm as weapons are poor teachers and unworthy of the trust placed in them. It does terrible harm to young lives. Don't be afraid to complain.

Overbusyness

Teenagers can feel discouraged just because they've become too busy. They're suffering from burn-out. It's amazing how much energy they can consume, not only with activity but also because their bodies are still growing. An endless round of meetings, social activities, sports and parties, coupled with a run of late nights, can be quite sufficient to produce a drop in spirits.

This is the time when you need to insist on some early nights and on some nights in. Never mind the complaints! They won't like it, but you'll probably find within a few weeks they're feeling much better and the spiritual sparkle is returning. Sometimes a few vitamins and some iron tablets for girls can help, too.

Secret sins

It's not unusual for youth leaders to have boys confessing to masturbation problems and feeling they've 'blown it' spiritually. The subject, as we've indicated earlier, needs to be openly and sensitively talked about.

It may be, of course, that they've been stumbled and let

down by the sins of others, notably people in the church. They may have picked up on unjust criticism or thoughtless speech. Because teenagers don't always get it right, some older folk are apt to convey to them that they've always got it entirely wrong. That can be very discouraging to youngsters. You have to deal with these matters, not simply by taking sides but by helping them to forgive—and by assisting them in seeing where they unwittingly offend others.

Where's God?

They might feel let down by God. We have to help our children understand what the Lord is doing with them when he appears not to answer their prayers. It can be confusing, to say the least.

One of our daughters has had a tough time with back trouble and has, on occasions, felt quite mystified about the will of God. She's gone forward at healing meetings where the speakers have claimed that God is moving by his Spirit and doing all sorts of wonderful things. People have laid hands on her. She's fallen down and shaken, rocked and rolled, or whatever else people do in these meetings, and still she's not healed!

Discouragement isn't very far off at such times and it requires of us wise counsel and support. Coping with apparently unanswered prayer is a problem for us all, and learning how to handle it is part of growing up in the Lord.

By and large, teenagers are robust creatures. They do get discouraged, but they have remarkable powers of recovery. Provided we are sensitive to their needs and are there at the right time, these phases soon pass. Only if depression becomes a way of life do we need to probe deeper and call in some outside help.

Just occasionally, discouragement can lead to open backsliding. It's a terrible pain for a parent to watch powerless as their child rebels against the faith and becomes just like his non-Christian school friends. A child in that state can become quite intolerable, perhaps blatantly smoking, swearing, blasting out the heavy rock; in fact demonstrating thoroughly that he has rejected the Lord.

What matters most in such unfortunate circumstances is that you continue to love your child. You will never win him back to God by withdrawing your affection. Love, self-restraint and prayer is the way. Like the father of the prodigal son, you must wait in faith. One day, you'll see in the distance a dust-covered figure drawing towards you....

The last word

The trouble with the last word is that it can't be written! There's always something more—especially when it comes to teenagers.

In Malachi 2:15, speaking of the marriage covenant, the prophet says, 'Has not the Lord made them one? In flesh and spirit they are his. And why one? Because he was seeking godly offspring.'

The most important thing that we will ever do is to pass on the flame of godliness to the next generation. Our most vital work is to produce future saints and servants of God.

We hope you've realised that this cannot be achieved in isolation from everything else. The relationship that we spoke about in the first section is crucial. We've also got to help them handle the reality of living in this world. We need to tackle this very big area of sexuality and sexual behaviour. We must stand with them in the process of discovering the will of God for their lives.

We didn't set out to answer all the questions or to provide an exhaustive manual on teen-rearing when we commenced this book. It can't be done. Rather, we've tried to suggest an approach, an outlook, and some guidelines to follow—along with a few pitfalls to avoid. We've sought to be sympathetic and encouraging. For all that, you may feel inadequate, not to say a bit of a failure.

Virtually every parent does at some point or other. And that should encourage us. There's no such creature as the perfect parent. What we have are a lot of people doing their best, not losing heart, managing these years, day by day as they come. Along the way there are times of success and times of failure. What we've modestly tried to do is provide the means of avoiding disaster with a bit of divine wisdom.

That, in the event, will prove sufficient. Follow the Lord's ways and your children will love you, even if at times they show it in strange ways. One day they will bless you for your firmness and your understanding—most of all because you were there and you cared.

So be encouraged, weary, wonderful pilgrim! God's grace is sufficient for this task. Pour your nerve tonic down the sink and pray. You'll be pleasantly surprised at the outcome. Indeed, it could turn out to be really good fun most of the time.

Psalm 145:3–4 declares, 'Great is the Lord and most worthy of praise; his greatness no-one can fathom. One generation will commend your works to another; they will tell of your mighty acts.'

God will help us to pass on this heritage to our children. Opposition abounds, but the Lord's power is perfected in weak but willing parents such as ourselves. Can we do it? In his strength we can.